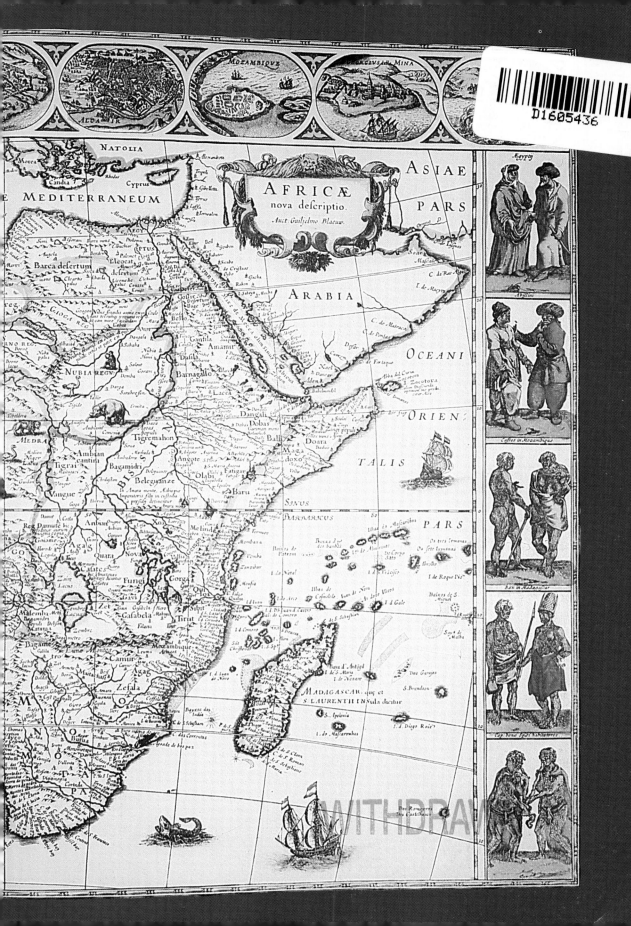

OUT OF AFRICA

I've known rivers:
I've known rivers ancient as the world and older than the flow
of human blood in human veins.
My soul has grown deep like the rivers.
I bathed in the Euphrates when dawns were young.
I built my hut near the Congo and it lulled me to sleep.
I looked upon the Nile and raised the pyramids above it. . . .
I've known rivers:
Ancient, dusky rivers.
My soul has grown deep like the rivers.

Langston Hughes
"The Negro Speaks of Rivers"

(Photo courtesy of the Museum of African Art, Eliot Elisofon Archives.)

OUT
OF
AFRICA

*From West African Kingdoms
to Colonization*

LOUISE DANIEL HUTCHINSON

Published for the
Anacostia Neighborhood Museum of the
Smithsonian Institution
by the
Smithsonian Institution Press
City of Washington
1979

First edition, 1979
Second printing, 1979

Cover: The Three Faces of Africa. (Courtesy of Howard University, Moorland-Spingarn Research Center.)
Frontispiece: River in Africa. (Courtesy of the Museum of African Art, Eliot Elisofon Archives.)

Endpapers: Map of Africa produced by the Dutch cartographer Willem Janszoon Blaeu (1642). (From *Africa on Maps Dating from the Twelfth to the Eighteenth Century . . .* by Egon Klemp.)

Permissions:
"The Negro Speaks of Rivers." From *Selected Poems of Langston Hughes.* Copyright © 1926 by Alfred A. Knopf, Inc. and renewed 1954 by Langston Hughes. Reprinted by permission of the publisher.

Quotations on page 45 from *The World and Africa* by W. E. B. Du Bois. Published by International Publishers (1965). Used by permission of the publisher.

Quotation on page 200 from *Africa Awake* by W. E. B. Du Bois (1958). Quoted in *W. E. B. Du Bois Speaks,* ed. by Philip S. Foner. Published by Pathfinder Press (1970). Used by permission of the publisher.

Maps on pages 21, 22, 25, 26, 29-31 are from *A History of West Africa* by Basil Davidson. Copyright © 1966 by Basil Davidson and Copyright © 1965 by Longmans, Green and Co. Ltd. Reproduced by permission of Doubleday & Company, Inc.

Library of Congress Cataloging in Publication Data
Hutchinson, Louise Daniel.
Out of Africa.
    Bibliography: p. 208
    Includes index.
    1. Africa, West—History. I. Anacostia
Neighborhood Museum. II. Title.
DT476.H87   966   78-22469
ISBN 0-87474-533-0

For sale by the Superintendent of Documents
United States Government Printing Office
Washington, D.C. 20402
Stock number 047-000-00357-1

Dedicated to the memory of two great Africanists:

W. E. B. Du Bois and William Leo Hansberry

Ex Africa semper aliquid novi.
(There is always something new out of Africa.)

—Pliny the Elder
  (A.D. 23-79)
  Natural History

CONTENTS

Foreword   *John R. Kinard* *11*

Acknowledgments *13*

Introduction   *Dr. Hollis R. Lynch* *15*

I. EARLY KINGDOMS AND INDEPENDENT STATES *19*
West African Beginnings *19*
Ancient Ghana *20*
Mali *22*
Songhai *24*
Timbuktu *26*
The Rise of Independent City-States *28*
   The Mossi States *28*
   Hausa States *29*
   Kanem-Bornu *31*
   The Akan *32*

II. THIS SUM OF ALL VILLAINIES:
SLAVERY AND THE SLAVE-TRADE SYSTEM *35*
The Spanish and Portuguese *35*
Slavery in Africa and the Western Hemisphere *40*

III. LET YOUR MOTTO BE RESISTANCE:
SLAVE REVOLTS IN THE CARIBBEAN AND THE UNITED STATES *45*
Prelude to Rebellion *45*
Toussaint L'Ouverture and the Caribbean *48*
Resistance in the United States *52*

IV. THE RETURN TO THE SOURCE:
THE ANTISLAVERY, ABOLITIONIST, AND COLONIZATION
MOVEMENTS *57*
Abolition and Colonial America *57*
England and the Colonization Movement *59*
The Founding of Liberia *61*

PICTORIAL ESSAY *71*
The Quest *71*
Ancient Kingdoms *80*
Art of West Africa *84*
The Slave Trade *91*
Slave Life in the Caribbean *102*
Slavery in the United States *106*
Resistance and Revolt *130*
Gaining Freedom *149*
The Abolitionists: Personalities and Documents *160*
The Pro-Colonization Movement *174*
The Anti-Colonization Movement *180*
Liberia *186*

EPILOGUE: WE THE CHILDREN OF AFRICA IN THIS LAND *200*

Lenders to the Exhibition and Catalogue *206*
Selected Bibliography *208*
Index *217*

FOREWORD

The lonesome soul cries out for that distant home that was yesterday, is today, and will forever be; and sighs Africa, Oh, My Africa! For out of Africa and cascading down the corridors of time have come earthshaking ideas, beautiful things, resources, riches, and people. Collectively they have made wealthy all the nations of the earth; for centuries past, and until this very day.

A mysterious continent, Africa has always aroused great interest, curiosity, and amazement. People of other nations and cultures have either been fascinated and enlivened or disturbed by the power of the richly hued African. Africa continues to be the faraway cultural and spiritual home for millions of black people here and in other corners of the earth, whose ancestors were bought, stolen, or ransomed as slaves. And while generations have believed that black ethnicity and ethno-history were lost, the glorious past like a sleeping giant has only been lying dormant. But now the great giant stirs, and today we stand on the threshold of a great renaissance. The ancestors are awakening.

Transported in the holds of slaving vessels, the influence of Africa, like a seed, has been sown and has been taking root in many lands of the Western Hemisphere, resulting in a cultural cross-fertilization. In varying degrees we now find indications of "African-ness" in the many places that black people reside. For some American blacks the continuing African presence has been disturbing and has resulted in a denial of their heritage. Preferring to imitate and emulate the majority culture in America, they have fallen victim to the "dark continent" myth.

At the beginning of the twentieth century, in *The Souls of Black Folk,* W. E. B. Du Bois prophetically wrote that the problem of this century would be the problem of the color line. He described the dilemma of the black American in this century as that of "twoness": the dilemma of the African personality struggling against subjugation and oppression in an assimilated Afro-American skin. But I think that it goes much deeper than pigmentation, for the psychic scars left by the experience of slavery have been slow to heal. And while adapting and assimilating out of a felt need to be accepted by the American majority culture, African descendants in America have gone through periods of self-hatred, self-rejection, and self-denial. Now is the time for self-enlightenment. Now is the time for rebirth.

If in fact the protest marches, freedom rides, sit-ins, kneel-ins, and pray-ins of the

1960s are to be more than a shallow victory, the black American must understand his history and heritage if he is to reshape his future. For while many Americans can feel confident about their past, for the black American the study of the past becomes a prime social necessity. As Arthur Schomburg has noted: "For the [African] American, a group tradition must [provide] compensation for persecution, and pride of race the antidote for prejudice. History must restore what slavery took away. For it is the social damage of slavery that the present generation must repair."

This catalogue and the exhibition it accompanies grew out of the legitimate and continuing quest to recover black history. For though blacks have been born on foreign soil, their desire for self-knowledge remains vital. Only this knowledge of self will supply the confidence to develop black abilities to the fullest and to soar to the cultural heights of African-ness.

We must see in this document and the exhibition it accompanies, an heroic past, where oppression is met by an unconquerable and unrelenting spirit and where the struggle to survive produces creative ingenuity. The catalogue presents a rich documentation of black history, and it is to be hoped that each who has access to it will find here information that both inspires and challenges. For the task for this and succeeding generations is to take the best of the past and the present and make for all humanity a glorious future—a future that will be shared by those who remain "the children of Africa in this land."

John R. Kinard
Director,
Anacostia Neighborhood Museum
February 1979

ACKNOWLEDGMENTS

Simply stated, history is the story of man and the record of his relationships with his environment and other people. In an effort to reach our objective of producing a document and an exhibit that would be readable and informative for both the student of history and the layman, we are indebted to librarians, curators, and archivists, many of whom responded to our written queries for assistance. For most, it was their first acquaintance with the Anacostia Neighborhood Museum. For the Museum's research staff, it was a challenge and an opportunity to bring together such a rich and varied collection of primary source materials.

We think that this catalogue and the exhibit it accompanies offer a unique opportunity to touch history. Each document, photograph, and art object has been selected for the poignant story it tells, and like the printed word is meant to be read. Each authenticates and conclusively tells a part of the story of Africans and their Afro-American descendants. For many months now, we have worked toward this end.

This research project generated a tremendous amount of work for a staff so small, and without the cooperation of many people and institutions neither the catalogue nor the exhibit would have been possible. In an effort to include all contributors, we have listed lending institutions separately. However, inevitably there are some that we feel a special indebtedness to, and among them are: Harvard University and its photographic curator Mr. Daniel Jones, for carefully preparing the reproductions of the Louis Agassiz slave daguerreotypes; the staff of the Manuscripts Department of the University of Virginia Library, for bringing the Robert T. Hubard slave journal to our attention, and for granting permission to photocopy the slave records published in Thomas Jefferson's *Farm Book;* Dr. S. Dillon Ripley, for assisting in obtaining permission from the United States Senate to exhibit and publish the congressional act authorizing Paul Cuffe to sail with cargo to Sierra Leone; the Rutgers University manuscripts collection staff, for aiding in the identification of the Peter Still collection; and Dr. John Buffington and Mrs. Agnes Sherman at Penn Community Services, Inc., St. Helena's Island, Frogmore, South Carolina, for permitting us to use the rich material from the Center's photographic collection. We wish to thank the South Carolina Department of Archives and History for assistance in locating the will of John Deas; Yale University for permission to publish life sketches from its collection of portraits of the *Amistad* captives; Mr. Leon H. Brody of the Rhode Island Black Heritage Society, for information on Thomas Howland; and Dr. Leonard Jeffries, City College of New York, and his wife Rosalyn, for the two days they spent with the Museum's staff, helping us to understand the impact of Africa on world history. We also wish to thank the staff of the Joseph Henry Papers, Smithsonian Institution, who with only a fragment of information, located correspondence to Joseph Henry from Alexander Crummell and Edward Blyden regarding colonization efforts in Liberia. Still other branches of the Smithsonian Institution have generously lent artifacts from their collections.

Thanks are extended to Mr. Thomas Battle, Mrs. Esme Bhan, and Ms. Maricia Battle of Howard University's Moorland-Springarn Research Center, for assistance in locating material. To Dr. Hollis R. Lynch, who prepared the introduction in spite of academic responsibilities and travel schedules; to Dr. Benjamin Quarles, who made valuable suggestions concerning the chapter on slavery and the slave trade; and to Mr. Terry D. Coleman, a community resident and a member of the Museum board, who brought information about blacks in Rhode Island to our attention and who read the complete manuscript and made helpful criticisms, we are especially grateful. We also thank Mrs. Winifred Johns, a community resident and teacher in the D.C. public schools, who reviewed the manuscript for readability and general interest level. Thanks are also due to Louise Heskett, editor, at the Smithsonian Institution Press.

As the Museum's historian, I would like to extend a very special thanks to all the staff of the Anacostia Neighborhood Museum, but particularly to the staff of the Research Department. Here, I acknowledge my indebtedness and gratitude to the Department's secretary Mrs. Hazelene Evans, who continuously typed correspondence to more than sixty repositories, ordered all research materials, kept track of all expenditures, arranged for inter-library loans, and typed the manuscript. My thanks are also extended to Miss Carolyn Margolis, who selected prints from the Museum of African Art, assisted with the organization of all illustrative materials, and prepared the index to the catalogue; also to our project editor Mr. John C. Harris, who did the initial editing of the manuscript, helped with the organization of prints, and assisted with the preparation of the bibliography and the index. I would like to thank Mr. Norman Rhodes, the Museum's staff photographer, who prepared all black-and-white illustrations; I would also like to acknowledge the continued cooperation of Mr. Sterling Jones and the staff of the Smithsonian Institution's Office of Printing and Photographic Services, with special thanks to Mrs. Hannelore "Lore" Aceto for the color reproduction work. And a special thanks to Mr. Jack F. Marquardt, Chief, Access Services, Smithsonian Institution Library, and his staff for their continued assistance in obtaining books and microfilm, some through Interlibrary Loan, for use in this research project.

Finally, I am especially grateful to Mr. John R. Kinard, the Museum's director, for his continued confidence and encouragement.

INTRODUCTION

West Africa, from Senegal to the Cameroons, from whence derived the vast majority of the ancestors of blacks today in the United States and the Caribbean, has been, in historic times, a populous, complex, vital area rich in history and unsurpassed in its artistic creations in wood sculpture and bronze. Here iron technology and agriculture had developed early, leading to a large sedentary population. The first major links to the outside world came via the vast trans-Saharan trade in goods and ideas. It was primarily this trade with North Africa which provided the stimulus for the establishment of the succession of three major empires in the Western Sudan—Ghana, Mali, and Songhai—spanning the period from the eighth to the sixteenth century. From North Africa, too, came Islamic religion and learning. From about the eleventh century on, most of the emperors of the Western Sudan were at least nominally Muslim. Islamic studies and scholarship flourished in such major centers as Jenne and Timbuktu. However, it was not until the nineteenth century that Islam spread to the masses of West Africans, and today somewhat more than fifty percent of them are Muslims.

European contact with West Africa began with the Portuguese in the second half of the fifteenth century, and they were followed by other Europeans, notably the Dutch, the British, and the French. The Europeans had to contend directly or indirectly with such well-organized West African coastal forest states as Dahomey, Oyo, Benin, and Ashanti, and for more than three centuries their activities were confined very largely to the coast. Unfortunately, European activities came to focus overwhelmingly on the trade in African slaves to meet the enormous demand for labor on the plantations of the Americas. To facilitate the slave trade, the Europeans erected forts, castles, and slave barracoons on the coast. The European-stimulated slave trade brought widespread devastation, death, and insecurity to West Africans. It has been estimated that some 10,000,000 Africans came to the Americas via the slave trade. It is likely that a similar number died from wars induced by the slave trade, the long, hard trek to the coast, and the conditions in the crowded, stinking holds of the slave ships in the dreaded "Middle Passage." The transatlantic slave trade has been one of the monumental atrocities of modern history.

In the Americas an equally hard lot awaited the slaves. The typical slave was a field hand on a sugar, rice, indigo, or cotton plantation. He was exploited systematically and sometimes worked to death. He was almost completely at the whim of his master, with few or no rights, without privacy, and without the opportunity for a stable family life. For its survival, the system of slavery required swift and harsh reprisals against those who challenged it. A wide, brutal, and ingenious range of punishments for the rebellious often resulted in their maiming or death.

Nonetheless, the slaves demonstrated their humanity and their intrinsic love of freedom by fighting with the weapons at their disposal: deceptive obsequiousness; malingering; destruction of property; plots and revolts such as those of Gabriel Prosser, Denmark Vesey, and Nat Turner; and by running away, well exemplified by the Maroons of Jamaica. Thus abolitionism began among the slaves themselves. But it became a major organized movement led by free blacks and sympathetic whites. Everywhere in the slave societies of the Americas a free black class, often the product of widespread miscegenation, had grown up. These free blacks were considerably more numerous, and had larger roles to play, in Latin than in Anglo-Saxon America.

In the United States the free black group constituted ten percent of the entire black population. In the English colonies in America, deliberate steps were taken to keep to a minimum the free black population, lest it pose a threat to the institution of slavery. A free black group had come into being primarily from the early African indentures and from blacks set free for their military service to the state, notably during the American Revolutionary War. Indeed, after independence, slavery in the North, which had never developed deep roots as its climate was unsuited to the plantation economy, gradually died out, terminating altogether by the end of the third decade of the nineteenth century. The free black group was about equally divided between the North and the South. In the South, where slavery continued until the Civil War, free blacks were effectively muzzled, circumscribed, and controlled. But in the North, although discriminated against socially, economically, and politically, they became highly vocal and well organized. From the late eighteenth century, they began to organize separate institutions: churches, schools, and benevolent, fraternal, and mutual societies. They became obsessed with bringing an end to slavery and with winning full rights as citizens of the United States. They were among the founders and active members of the Underground Railroad, which spirited slaves from Southern plantations to physical freedom in the North. Through their newspapers, from their pulpits, through local, state, and national conventions, they fought arduously for abolition and freedom.

Some free blacks saw the solution to the general plight of blacks in the return of a select number among them to Africa. By helping to build one or more Christian, modern nations in West Africa, they hoped to bring an end to the slave trade; they also hoped to end slavery in the Americas by diplomatic means and economic competition. This thinking was stimulated by the founding of Sierra Leone in the late eighteenth century, under English auspices, by blacks from Britain, Nova Scotia, and Jamaica. Freetown, Sierra Leone's capital, had by the early nineteenth century become the major westernized center in West Africa. It was also the headquarters of the British attempt to end the slave trade, which the British and the United States governments, as much for economic as humanitarian reasons, had outlawed in 1807. Sierra Leone attracted the attention of Afro-Americans, including Paul Cuffe, the wealthy trader and shipowner from Massachusetts, who made two trips there in 1811 and 1815. Directly as a result of Cuffe's visits, the American Colonization Society, comprised of the "strange bedfellows" of humanitarians and slaveholders, was founded in 1817 to colonize "free people of color" in West Africa. Understandably, the motives of the Society for colonizing blacks in West Africa were not the same as those of blacks advocating repatriation: the former wanted to rid the United States of an unwanted element, the latter saw returning as the first step in a strategy to end the slave trade, slavery, and discrimination. The American Colonization Society provoked bitter opposition on the part of most free blacks and led to an acrimonious division in the Afro-American community between those who opposed and those who supported its activities. The Society and its Afro-American supporters were responsible for the establishment of Liberia, beginning in 1822. By the outbreak of the Civil War in the United States more than 15,000 emigrants had settled in Liberia, which in 1847 had become independent as a sovereign black republic. But the pan-African vision of cooperation between Afro-Americans and indigenous Africans in a vital and progressive Liberia did not materialize. Liberia, fighting against incredible odds, remained weak; its political independence was premature and unviable. Reprehensibly, the Afro-American emigrants scorned and exploited Africans and excluded them from political, economic, and social power. Afro-Americans themselves became ambivalent about Liberia; even its well-wishers regarded it with some embarrassment.

If neither the domestic nor the pan-African programs of Afro-Americans for freedom and dignity was having much success, despite valiant efforts, nonetheless, an end to slavery and the gain of constitutional citizenship did come as a result of the Civil War and its aftermath. Sectional slavery had put enormous strain on the new nation with democratic ideals. The Civil War resolved this contradiction with the victory of the North, bringing an end to slavery. Afro-Americans played a significant role in achieving that victory and their own freedom.

Thus after the painful passage from West Africa to America, and after the long and arduous odyssey of slavery, Afro-Americans had achieved a triumph over despotism and barbarity with the ending of slavery. But they were soon to learn that this was merely the end of the first stage in a prolonged battle for freedom and dignity. Theirs has been a history of struggle, endurance, and heroism. Along the road, they have won significant additional victories, but complete freedom is still to be attained. In their further struggle, they could and should derive inspiration from the past.

Hollis R. Lynch
Professor of History,
Columbia University
February 1979

I. EARLY KINGDOMS AND INDEPENDEN▲

The spell has been broken.
The buried treasures of antiquity again revisit the sun.

LEO FROBENIUS, *German*
scholar and explorer
1910.

WEST AFRICAN BEGINNINGS

West Africa is a region encompassing some two million square miles. Stretching from the Volta and Niger rivers—including the Gulf of Benin—and from the Atlantic Ocean to the Kong Mountains, lay fertile lands that fostered the growth and development of early African civilizations. The rivers that watered these regions were as essential to West Africa's history as the Nile River had been to Egypt's. Robin Hallett in his *Africa to 1875* provides a description.

> Spectacular as natural features [were] the . . . Senegal, Gambia, Volta, and above all, Niger with its extraordinary course, rising little more than two hundred miles from the sea, flowing northeastward to brush the fringes of the desert before completing its great bend by a south-easterly course across the savanna and the forest to the labyrinthine creeks and mangrove swamps of its long-mysterious delta.

The network of rivers and waterways defied foreign intrusion. And until the successful penetration of the African interior by Dr. David Livingstone and Henry Stanley, it was generally conceded that Africa had no past comparable to that of western civilizations. The inaccessibility of the interior contributed to Europe's ignorance of the region and gave rise to the "dark continent" myth. As late as the second decade of the twentieth century, A. P. Newton, a respected British professor, could claim that Africa had had *no* history before the arrival of the Europeans. Yet West African kingdoms and empires were flourishing nine hundred years before Newton made his sweeping declaration. Some historians believe that the ancient kingdoms may even have been in existence at the time of Christ.

The history of many of the black African societies and cultures can be traced to the discovery of agriculture. The diffusion of this new knowledge from east to west across the vast continent made possible the production of food for the masses of people and was directly related to the spread of the Iron Age.

First emerging among Asian people, the knowledge of iron-making was probably introduced to Africa in the seventh century, when Assyria conquered Egypt. Iron-making required an abundant supply of iron ore and timber. Egypt had neither ufficient amounts. Ancient Nubia, with an ample supply of both, became the first African kingdom to engage in iron-making. In this way, Africa advanced directly from the Stone Age to the Iron Age, without the usual transition from stone to copper and bronze—a unique feature of African history.

With the use of iron, a pastoral and nomadic life-style gave way to an agrarian one. The ability to smelt, fashion, and use iron caused African civilizations to advance rapidly. New technological skills and capabilities served as a catalyst for a new social and political order, and early West African kingdoms began to emerge.

One of the greatest of the early kingdoms was Ancient Ghana. Ghana—not to be confused with the modern nation of the same name—was located in what is now Mali and southern Mauritania. For several hundred years it was the strongest West African empire. It began to decline in the eleventh century, only to be succeeded by Mali, located in what are now Guinea and Mali. Mali in turn rose and fell, and in the late 1400s and early 1500s the Songhai empire succeeded it in strength and power.

The development of trade routes and the ability to competitively engage in commerce were essential to the building of these nations. Ancient Ghana and the other early kingdoms particularly depended on the trans-Saharan trade, which linked them with the port cities of the Mediterranean Sea and, ultimately, with Europe. On this vital trade network, gold and salt were the principal commodities. Ivory was also much sought after. In exchange, West Africans received the much-valued salt, copper, silks, metalware, ornamental bottles, jewelry, and bowls and lamps of bronze and silver. Later, the Islamic faith, together with spices and—still later—slaves, would also cross the Sahara on this great trade route.

Trade and commerce created new demands and markets for skilled artisans and craftsmen. Working in leather, woods, ivory, and precious metals, these craftsmen bolstered the economy, while other Africans worked the land to meet the needs of a growing population. Most importantly, the participation of the Africans themselves in an international trade network led to the founding of cities, many of which were trading centers near navigable waterways. As these settlements grew in population and importance, forms of government emerged. Extending their sphere of power and influence, cities developed into states. As smaller and weaker units came under their control and began to pay tribute, kingdoms and empires arose, thus making necessary laws and a centralized system of government. While often delegating authority to lesser officials, the ruler remained supreme. Taxes, derived largely from duties imposed on imports and exports, were levied to support the cost of government, and obedience was essential for the maintenance of order among the subjects.

Throughout the period of nation-building, the people of West Africa adopted new socio-economic alliances and new political allegiances. The histories of these new West African states resemble one another: they were, after all, responding to similar geographical, social, and political conditions.

ANCIENT GHANA

A strong trading center before the ninth century, the earliest large city-state of West Africa was Aoukar, the area later known as Ancient Ghana. (''Ghana'' is a title

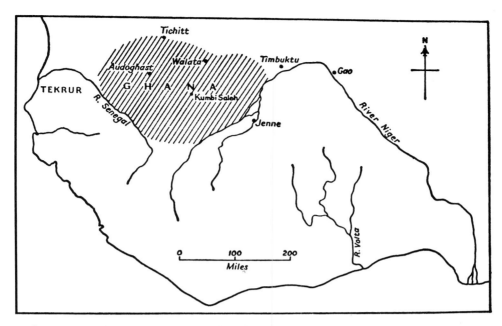

Ancient Ghana. This great kingdom was at its height around the year 1000.

meaning "war chief" that was conferred on the ruler of the country.) Located between the headwaters of the Senegal and Niger rivers, the kingdom flourished until the eleventh century.

Reaching its zenith by A.D. 1000, Ghana had succeeded in bringing a number of smaller states under its domination. It monopolized the West African gold trade, exporting to North Africa and Europe, and its armies controlled the roads leading to the major cities and centers of commerce. During this time, Ghana was described as an empire with two important cities. One was inhabited by Muslim traders, with twelve mosques; the other by the emperor and the indigenous tribes.

The power and influence of Ghana began to decline about the second half of the eleventh century. Ibn Hawqal, a tenth-century writer, had once described Ghana's ruler as "the wealthiest of all kings on the face of the earth on account of the riches he owns and the hoards of gold acquired by him and inherited from his predecessors since ancient times." But the king now fell into disfavor with his people. The empire weakened from within, thus making it vulnerable to attack from without. In the year 1020, North African forces launched an unsuccessful offensive against Ghana, and by 1042 the Almoravids had begun a systematic attack on the kingdom's outlying districts.

The Almoravids, a Muslim-Berber dynasty, came from the city of Adrar in Mauritania in northwestern Africa. Following a pilgrimage to Mecca about 1049, Yahya inbn-Ibrahim, the chief of the Berbers, retreated to an island near the Senegal coast. There, with advisor Abdallah ibn-Yasin—Muslim preacher—the Berber chief engaged in daily prayer and meditation and began raising a military force. Described as a fortified monastery, the settlement was called "Almoravids," and the people who took part in a contemporary holy war were soon identified by the same name.

Attacking the caravan center of Sidjulmassa (Sijilmasa) where Ghanaian gold merchants went to barter and palaver with the North African and Arab traders, the Almoravids succeeded in disorganizing trade relations and creating dissension among those who paid tribute to Ghana. This in turn weakened the centralized government, which was based on a standard of gold. With the plunder in 1055 of Awdaghast (Audoghast), a Ghanaian dependent state, the decline of Ancient Ghana was imminent. United by Abu Bakr Ibn-Umar, the Almoravids finally conquered Ghana in 1076, and the people were forced to convert to the Islamic faith.

The Almoravids, though, were unable to hold the land and the allegiance of those they had conquered, and their new empire was short-lived. Abu Bakr's death in 1087 resulted in a serious challenge to the control and authority of the Almoravids. That same year the Ghanaian empire collapsed. Though its culture would remain a powerful presence for two more centuries, Ghana's political and economic influence had come to an end.

MALI

Through rock paintings and carvings, archeologists and anthropologists have been able to date the history of the area known as Mali back to prehistoric times. But it was not until the thirteenth century that it rivaled Ancient Ghana in power and became the second-largest West African kingdom.

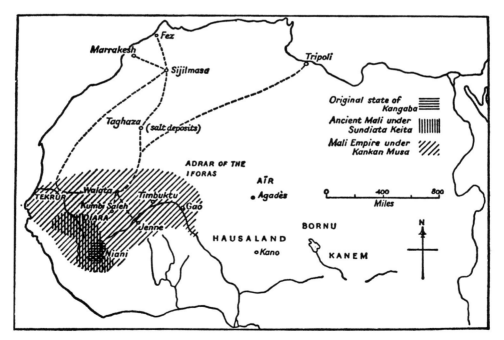

The expansion of the empire of Mali. Mansa Kankan Musa, Mali's greatest king, ruled from about 1307 to 1337. As this map shows, during his reign Mali reached its zenith.

Mali, meaning "where the king lives," was inhabited by the Malinke and Mandingo peoples. This empire covered a vast territory that stretched from the Atlantic Ocean on the west to the Senegal River on the east. While its beginnings are obscure, it is known that by the middle of the eleventh century the people of the region had embraced Islam.

Taking complete control of Ghana's gold-producing provinces of Senegal and Bouré, Mali also gained the monopoly on the caravan trade in gold dust. Since the source of the gold was an ancient secret, the North African and Arab traders had no recourse but to engage in commerce and trade with the new power.

About 1307, Mansa Kankan Musa ascended to the throne. Known as "Mansa Musa"—"mansa" meaning "emperor"—the king established himself as the greatest ruler of Mali. In 1324 he made an historic pilgrimage to Mecca, and the splendor of his retinue was described as follows:

> The huge caravan included . . . 12,000 slaves, all dressed in brocade and Persian silk. Mansa Musa himself rode on horseback. . . . Directly preceding him were 500 slaves, each carrying a staff of gold weighing about 6 pounds. Then came Mansa Musa's baggage—a train of 80 camels, each carrying 300 pounds weight of gold dust.

En route to Mecca, the sovereign himself distributed alms and gifts to the poor. Returning to Mali, and following the establishment of diplomatic relations with Morocco and Egypt, Mansa Musa invited Arab scholars and traders to Mali. It was from these men that Europe first learned of Timbuktu as a center of learning and culture, a reputation that was to last longer than the Mali empire itself.

Mansa Musa's authority extended some five hundred miles in each direction. A Mandingo king and the grandson of Sundiata, the king of Ghana, Mansa Musa was respected and beloved for his justice and humanity. As the fame and fortune of his kingdom spread and Mali was recognized as a world power, European cartographers began to make maps depicting Mali, Gao, and Timbuktu. A fourteenth-century map shows Mansa Musa and the Mali empire and includes the following caption: "This negro [sic] lord is called Musa Mali [sic], lord of the Negroes of Guinea. So abundant is the gold which is found in his land that he is the richest and most noble king in all the land."

Mali's fame, peace, and fortune were soon to be attacked by covetous neighbors. With the fall of the major cities of Walata and Timbuktu to the Tuaregs on the north and the capture of territory on the south of the Mossi, Mali was severely weakened. Its decline continued after the death of Mansa Musa about 1337. For twenty-five years Mansa Musa had ruled justly and skillfully. His followers and successors, lacking his traits of leadership, were only able to hold the empire together until about 1400.

By the fifteenth century, the Portuguese had begun their navigation and exploration of Africa's west coast. It is indeed paradoxical that Mali turned to Portugal for help in an effort to halt the annexing of her lands, the raids along her borders, and the subjugation of her people. The Portuguese, not wanting to alienate any potential partners in trade, responded by sending only a diplomatic mission. Later, the Mandingo would seek assistance from Portugal in hopes of rebuilding their empire, only to find themselves enslaved by the Portuguese and other Europeans.

By the middle of the seventeenth century Mali had been reduced to its original size, to the area called "Kangaba." Its decline resulted from the growth of trade in the area—and subsequent trade rivalries—and the strengthening of the concepts of kingship and centralized government. These and similar influences powerfully affected many other peoples in West Africa.

SONGHAI

As is true of other civilizations, mythology has been intricately woven into the fabric of West African history. As-Sadi, the seventeenth-century historian, is credited with recording and preserving the following legend, a mythical account of the origin of the Songhai dynasty:

> A stranger known as Za al-Ayaman, 'the man from Yemen,' came to the ancient town of Kukia on the Niger, found the people being terrorized by a fish, killed the monster, was gratefully accepted by the people as their ruler, and thus became the founder of the first Songhai dynasty.

More factual accounts tell us that, displacing the Sorko people who lived there, the Songhai (Songhay) established themselves at the city of Gao in about the seventh century. As Gao began to extend its power and influence, its importance as a trade center was recognized. When Mansa Musa rose to power, he dispatched his armies to annex Songhai and bring it under his dominion, thereby making it a tributary to Mali.

The vastness of Mali proved to be unmanageable, and its control over Gao and the Songhai was not to last for very long. Regaining their independence about 1375, the Songhai themselves began a program of expansion. In 1464, during a time of turmoil within the kingdom, a military and political leader known as Sunni Ali ascended to power. His goal was to unify the kingdom, establish laws and a centralized government, and peacefully strengthen the nation's economy. Beginning his reign in 1464, Sunni Ali is recognized as the founder of the Songhai empire, which soon rivaled Mali in both size and influence. Prospering, the new empire now controlled the gold, ivory, and salt trades of the Western Sudan.

When Sunni Ali died late in the fifteenth century, Songhai was reaching its zenith. Amassing even more land, and annexing smaller communities of city-states, Songhai's program of nation-building was continued by Sunni Ali's son, Sunni Baru. Defeated in battle and ruling for only one year, Sunni Baru was deposed and replaced by Askia Muhammad (who was also known as Muhammad Turé). Askia Muhammad was a legendary figure who came to be known as "Askia the Great." His reign of thirty-six years as the emperor of Songhai has been described as momentous and triumphant.

Ruling from 1493 until 1528, Askia, as did Sunni Ali before him, found government officials engaged in disputes resulting from personal ambitions and religious differences. The Islamic merchant class in the large trade centers had begun to

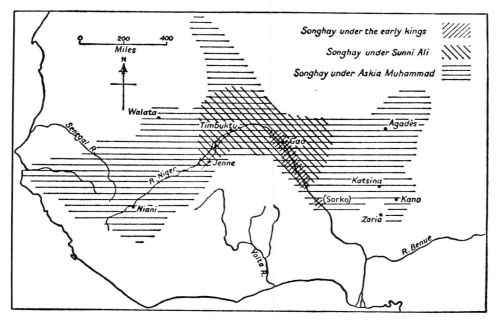

The expansion of the empire of Songhai (Songhay).

influence the affairs of government. Yet in direct conflict with Islamic beliefs, discord was spreading across the Western Sudan. At the same time, import and export taxes were needed to keep revenue flowing into the empire's coffers. Askia's predecessors had deemed it wise and expedient to make concessions to Islam. To maintain a balance of trade relations, it was essential that the interests of both the Islamic trade centers and the non-Islamic farming people be protected.

Refusal by Sunni Baru to adopt the Islamic faith had alienated the powerful tradesmen and resulted in his downfall. Recognizing the political influence of the trade centers, Askia Muhammad, at age fifty, broke with family tradition and converted to the Islamic faith. Askia, however, was a tolerant man, and many indigenous and traditional customs continued to be practiced in his court. But in all matters pertaining to trade and government, his laws reflected the acceptance of Islamic ideas and beliefs.

A two-year pilgrimage to Mecca reaffirmed Askia Muhammad's belief in the correctness of his administrative decisions. Upon his return to Songhai, he began to reorganize the government along stricter Muslim lines. Adopting and strengthening many of the policies instituted by Sunni Ali, Askia the Great developed and perfected a system of government that was acknowledged to be more powerful and more complex than that of any other state in the area. Skillfully bringing his knowledge of politics and military strategy to bear, Askia extended Songhai's influence farther north and into the marketplaces of the Sahara.

Throughout the Western Sudan, the exploits of Askia Muhammad's cavalry and armies were much celebrated and feared. The Mossi of Yatenga, the Futa Toro in faraway Senegal, and the Hausa states, had felt his might. Conquests were made in the name of Islam. By the end of Askia Muhammad's reign in 1528, the power of Songhai had reached the cities along the Niger River, giving the empire control of the caravan routes leading to the north and to European markets.

The decline of Songhai was directly related to the rejection of the Islamic faith by Askia Musa, the eldest son of Askia Muhammad. After reigning for only three years, Askia Musa was killed by his subjects. He was succeeded by a number of rulers who were unable to restore Songhai to its place of respect in the world community. The process of deterioration accelerated. Internal strife and disorder were accompanied by revolts and raids along the borders.

With the arrival of the Portuguese and the fall of Gao and Timbuktu to Moroccan invaders, the strong authority of the Songhai government collapsed. The decline of the Songhai empire paralleled the diminishing influence of Islam in government.

TIMBUKTU

Neither a kingdom nor an independent state, Timbuktu was an important trade center at the headwaters of the Niger River. As the unrivaled and undisputed seat of West African culture and a significant part of the Mali and Songhai empires, this city of legendary fame deserves a special place in the annals of African history. While only vestiges of its former glory remain, yet with the mosque of Mansa Kankan Musa and the tomb of Askia the Great nestled among its dusty ruins, Timbuktu continues to hold memories of Africa's great past.

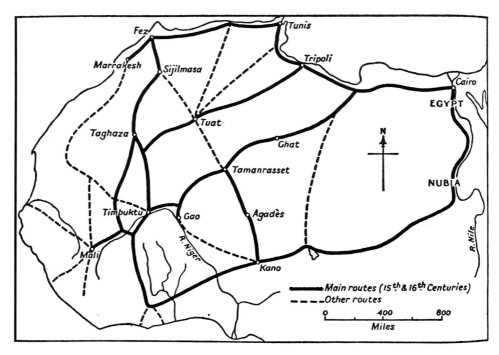

Caravan routes across the Sahara in the fifteenth and sixteenth centuries.

Felix Dubois's sentiments—written after a visit to Timbuktu in 1897—are a clear indication of the city's place in world history:

> Askia the Great made Timbuctoo one of the world's great centers of learning and commerce. The brilliance of the city was such that it still shines in the imagination after three centuries like a star which, though dead, continues to send its light toward us. Such was its splendor that in spite of its many vicissitudes after the death of Askia, the vitality of Timbuctoo is not extinguished.

Founded about 1100, Timbuktu was one of the richest commercial cities in West Africa. Its site near the southern boundary of the Sahara and about ten miles north of the Niger River was ideal for the conduct of trade. Early recorders of its history described Timbuktu as the "meeting point of camel and canoe." There, goods from North Africa were exchanged for commodities from the forests and grasslands of West Africa. Camel caravans from North Africa carried salt, cloth, copper, dates and figs, and metalwares to Timbuktu. The resident merchants of Timbuktu traded gold, ivory, kola nuts, and slaves.

Although its fame as a trading center spread from east to west across the continent, Timbuktu was inadequately located to become a capital city. Vulnerable to attack, during its history the city changed hands many times. Mansa Musa brought it under the dominion of Mali, and Askia the Great made it a tributary to the Songhai empire. Later, it was conquered and its people subjugated by the Tuareg nomads of the Sahara, the Moroccans, and the Tukular empire. Although its government and political structure changed frequently, Timbuktu did enjoy periods of peace and prosperity. Despite changing alliances and allegiances, the political life of the city seemed not to impinge upon the network of cultural institutions which flourished for centuries.

After a visit to Timbuktu in the early 1500s, Leo Africanus[1] wrote:

> There are numerous judges, professors, and holy men, all being handsomely maintained by the king, who holds scholars in much honour. Here, too, they sell many handwritten books from North Africa. More profit is made from selling books in Timbuktu than from any other branch of trade.

Timbuktu also played a pivotal role in the preservation of West African history. Early writings about Africa were mostly in Arabic and were confined almost exclusively to the regions closest to the Mediterranean and the Red Sea. As Arab influence spread south, deeper into the continent, Arab scholars began to record the history of these territories. In Timbuktu, in the sixteenth and seventeenth centuries, the writing of history began to develop as a discipline and started to spread to regions bordering on the world of Islam. This transmission of knowledge was im-

---

[1]Leo Africanus's given name was Al-Hasan ibn Muhammad al-Wazzan as-Zayyati. He first visited the ancient city of Timbuktu at age fifteen, in the company of an uncle who was a Moroccan ambassador. He returned again while serving as a diplomat in the service of the king of Fez in Morocco. Captured in 1518, he was presented as a gift to Pope Leo X. That same year he was baptized and given the name of Giovanni Leo de' Medici, after his patron.

Tomb of Askia the Great.

measurably aided by the geographers and mapmakers of the period, who gave the world its first knowledge of "the land of the blacks."

It was also in Africa that ethno-history first emerged as an important discipline. In Timbuktu scholars collected oral histories and examined myths about the origins of the African past. These early studies included the examination of legends, semi-legendary traditions, and traditions more clearly derived from the generations immediately preceding their own. Archeological, linguistic, anthropological, and sociological evidences were also considered. Mahmoud Kati, a West African, was among the earliest practitioners of ethno-history. In 1519 he published *Tarikh el Fettach,* one of the earliest histories of the Songhai, Mandingo, and Sarakole peoples.

THE RISE OF INDEPENDENT CITY-STATES

The Mossi States

About 1600, West African history entered a new phase, as the power of government was regained by non-Muslims, the proletariat, and the people of the countryside.

At first independent of outside influences, and with an internal communications system that fostered economic and cultural development, the Mossi and Hausa states came into being between 1000 and 1600, together with the state of Kanem-Bornu. The southern portion of Kanem predated the year 1000. Later, these states

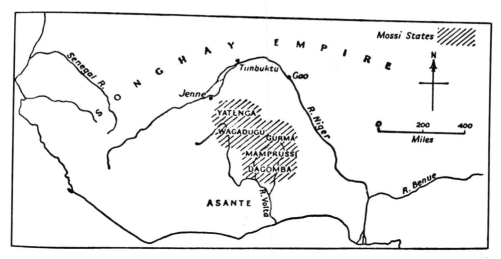

The Mossi states.

would also come in contact with Islam and become an important link in the trade routes connecting commercial centers.

Holding tenaciously to their religious and cultural beliefs, at first the Mossi states did not produce any goods for export. Migrating from the east between the eleventh and thirteenth centuries, during the next two centuries, the Mossi conducted highly successful raids on the wealthy trading cities along the Niger River. Such activities were eventually brought into check by the mighty armies of the Songhai empire. The Mossi later organized the territorial spoils of their conquest. From their excursions they acquired land that became the states of Tenkodogo, Yatenga, and Ouagadougou. Of the three, Ouagadougou became the most powerful.

Finally settling down to a life of commerce, the Mossi engaged in the trading of gold, kola nuts, and slaves, and they realized a great profit. By the eighteenth century, the Ashanti nation of Ghana had made significant inroads into the Mossi-held territory.

Hausa States

While the exact origin of the Hausa is obscure, the history of the Hausa lands is fairly well recorded and dates back to the tenth century. Among the early chroniclers of this history were ibn-Batutu[2] and Leo Africanus.

The first Hausa settlements were probably built during the tenth and eleventh centuries. Their populations gradually migrated west, and by the 1300s many Hausa

---

[2]A North African from the Luata tribe, ibn-Batutu (or Battuta) was born at Tangiers about 1304. Formally trained in theology, at age twenty-one he made a pilgrimage to Mecca, spending three years in study and devotion. Later, ibn-Batutu visited Africa's east coast, and as an emissary of the emperor of Delhi he met the Mongol Emperor of China. Absent from home for twenty-four years, he returned to Africa and visited the Mali empire. A learned scholar and a keen observer, ibn-Batutu left an important record of West African history. He died in North Africa about 1369.

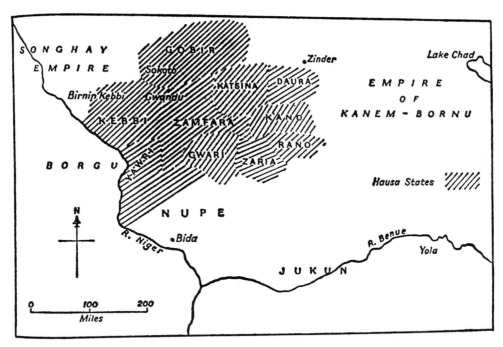

The Hausa states, a confederation that never developed a strong central government.

city-states had developed. Among them were Kano, Katsina, Sokoto, and Zaria. Although important as trade centers, the Hausa states never joined together as a confederation or established a strong central government.

The states had a highly developed economy. In addition to agriculture and the raising of cattle and horses, the Hausa were skilled in weaving and the making of jewelry.

In the thirteenth century the Hausa states came under the dominion of Mali, and they remained under its influence into the fourteenth century. In the fifteenth and sixteenth centuries the Songhai and Bornu both claimed sovereign rights over these states. Yet, while exacting taxes and tributes, neither Songhai nor Bornu seriously compromised the Hausa trade. The Hausa regained their independence for periods during the 1600s and 1700s, all the while continuing their trade in gold and slaves.

The Hausa lost their independence again in the early 1800s. Osman dan Fodio, a Fulani Muslim from Gobir, accused the Hausa of irreverence and waged a successful holy war against them. He ruled over the southern regions of the Hausa lands, and his son Ahmadu Bello ruled over the northern ones (now a part of Nigeria and Cameroon). Here Ahmadu Bello organized the Sokoto empire, which was later destroyed during the period of European exploration and conquest.

Since the Hausa enjoyed a reciprocal relationship with the Bornu, their political organization underwent very little change while under the control of the Bornu-based Fulani. Although the Fulani rulers were devout Muslims, the Hausa sovereign retained many of the sacred African customs and maintained a lavish court, with a large retinue of dependents.

Since the fourteenth century, all of the rulers of the Hausa lands had been practicing Muslims, yet strict adherence to Islamic laws was practiced only in the large trade centers. In the countryside, the populace retained the sacred practices of their local cultures. As skillful diplomats, the rulers understood the importance of Islam to the balance of trade; as Africans, they knew the need of the people to protect and retain their cultural identity. Thus, the Hausa lived most of their lives in a bicultural and pluralistic society.

Kanem-Bornu

Believed to have been founded between the seventh and tenth centuries, Kanem was one of the empires that flowered on the edge of the Sahara, in the Lake Chad region. Developing along a crossroads of commerce and migration, the Kanem empire, which included powerful city-states, covered much of the land area occupied today by the Republic of Chad.

Extending its influence from the Tibesti Mountains to the eastern shore of Lake Chad, the history of Kanem is closely linked to that of the kingdom of Bornu and the sultanate of Wadai, east of Kanem. Reportedly overthrown by the emerging Hausa in the tenth century, Kanem was invaded in the next century by the Teda of Tebesti, who annexed its lands and converted it to Islam.

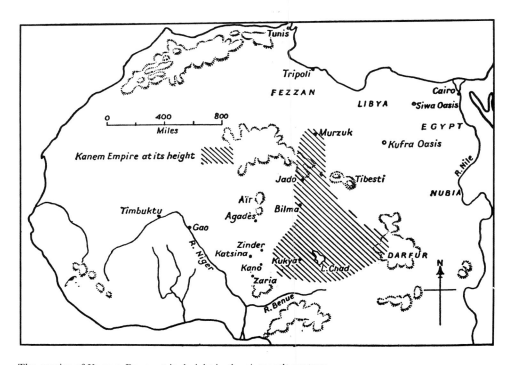

The empire of Kanem-Bornu at its height in the sixteenth century.

By the thirteenth century, the Kanembu, a black dynasty, had ascended to the throne and extended the frontiers of Kanem's kingdom to the borders of Tunisia and Egypt. As new groups in search of land migrated across the continent, Kanem's established communities became vulnerable to attack by rivals for their wealth and power. And in the following century the Bulala, who occupied land in the southeastern region of modern-day Chad, rebelled and deposed the ruling dynasty. Driven from Kanem, the members of the former ruling class were given asylum in the kingdom of Bornu.

Bornu was a black Muslim empire, and the extent of its power and influence was impressive. Spreading from the area known today as Nigeria, its influence extended through northern Cameroon and western Chad to southwestern Libya. The people of Bornu claimed a kinship to the Yemenite tribe, but historians believe that it is more probable that their empire was founded by nomadic Berbers from the Sahara. Despite its early conversion to Islam, its political organization and structure of government retained much of its African character and integrity.

The Bornu ruler, or ''Mai,'' was thought to be a divine king. Yet his powers were limited by ancestral customs and his reign shared with and supported by a queen mother. Uniquely, the king maintained a court with a dual hierarchy of functioning dignitaries, one free and the other slave. Together they combined and performed their duties at court, in concert with those of the provincial government.

The king of Bornu was a member of the Kanuri tribe, and as the one to which the ruling sovereign belonged it enjoyed a place of distinction and held a dominant position among the other tribes in the empire. Included among the peoples of Bornu were the Hausa, the Shuwa Arabs, the Fulani, the Mandara, and the Kotoko, who retained their own chief. These tribes maintained their linkage to the ruler through fealty, and sometimes personal bondage.

In the sixteenth century, with the annexation of Kanem as a province, Bornu reached a new height, then continued its program of territorial expansion into the next century. The combined influence and power of Kanem-Bornu were extended north as far as Kano (between Kokoto and Lake Chad in modern-day Nigeria). The annexation of Kanem resulted in disputes between the Bornu and the Wadai, and the rivalry and disagreements continued until the distribution of African territories among the colonial powers in 1800.

The decline of Kanem-Bornu began in the nineteenth century and was followed by serious economic, social, and political disorganization in the provinces. It was then conquered by the Sudanese slave trader Pahbah and finally divided into German, French, and English colonies, marking the demise of the state of Kanem-Bornu.

The Akan

For centuries there was a seemingly continuous migration across the African continent. Directly related to this movement was a cross-fertilization of civilizations that resulted in an assimilation process. The Akan give us an opportunity to see what the migration process involved and what changes it brought about in the socioeconomic and political life-style of a people. The Akan are typical of many nations that followed the trans-Saharan trade route—nations such as the Yoruba, the Mende, and the Senufo.

Beginning about the eleventh century, the migration of the Akan was probably accomplished in three distinct waves and probably accounts for the settling of southern Ghana and Asante.

The two main languages of the Akan people are Twi (an important literary language) and Fante. A third language, that of the Guan, is spoken in some areas conquered by the Akan, for this group retained its own language.

The Guan were the first of the Akan group to migrate southward into Ancient Ghana. They were followed by the Fante, and then by the Twi. The first peoples to relocate were called the Adanse, or "house builders." When the Portuguese arrived on the coast in 1471, the Akan had only recently arrived along the forest belt of the Western Sudan.

The early history of the Akan people has been studied from the vantage point of migration patterns, linguistic stock, and cultural heritage. The results have produced two very interesting hypotheses. While recognizing that the Akan were once a part of the kingdom of Ancient Ghana, one hypothesis proposes that this group relocated to the West African Gold Coast (modern-day Ghana, which is distinct from Ancient Ghana). The second hypothesis suggests that at least a part of this group migrated to the east and to the city-state of Kanem. As we shall see, both hypotheses may be correct.

The history of Abu Bakr and his Almoravid army in 1076 was a turning point in West African history. Causing the displacement of thousands of men, women, and children, it resulted in the southward march of several tribes then under the dominion of Ancient Ghana. It is believed that the Akan were among them. As they began their march, the Akan were probably unified politically and culturally. But by the time of their arrival on the borders of the Gold Coast, divisions had developed among the people. Three leaders were to emerge from among the divided groups: Osom, Oburumankuma, and Odapagyan. This triumvirate established the capital city of Mankessim.

But Mankessim was not the first city founded by the Akan in their new home. On the flatlands of the countryside and on the periphery of the forest, the Akan communally raised the city of Techiman. This relocation required a significant modification in the life-style of these people. After leaving the familiar savanna land—the tropical or subtropical grasslands—the Akan had to become acclimated to life in the forest belt. The familiar plow used in cultivating the land was replaced by new implements: the axe, cutlass, and hoe. The presence of the deadly tsetse fly (indigenous to Africa in regions south of the Sahara) made it virtually impossible for the Akan to continue their agricultural way of life, since cattle and horses could not survive in the new environment.

Studies of the Akan people have noted significant similarities between this group and the people who now inhabit modern-day Ghana, thus giving credibility to the stories of their migration. In the Akan society, much like that of Ghana, "Mother-right" prevailed in the city, and those who succeeded to positions of influence and power did so through the children of their sisters. Also like the Ghanaians, the Akan resisted Islam. Yet the progenitors of modern Ghana are known to be Mandingos, and there is no conclusive evidence of a kinship between the Akan and the Mandingos. Further research will have to be done on the question.

While some of the Akan probably settled in what is now western Ghana as early as the eleventh century, another group believed to be a part of the Akan people migrated to the Lake Chad region. Their culture seems to have been identical to that of the Akan. Further, they spoke a similar language and bore strikingly similar physical characteristics. Since the Akan women frequently accompanied their men into battle, with the fall of Ancient Ghana it is possible that entire family groups and clans fled the area. Relocating in and about Kanem, later they were forced to leave by the conquering Almoravids. If the hypothesis of J. C. DeGraft-Johnson[3] is correct, then the Akans, wandering from east to west, were finally reunited with their kinsmen among the forest lands of the West African Gold Coast, in today's Ghana.

---

[3]Until recent times, there were few native Africans who were scholars of African history. A Ghanaian by birth and a member of the Department of Economics at the University of Ghana, J. C. DeGraft-Johnson is one of this new breed of African scholars.

II. THIS SUM OF ALL VILLAINIES
Slavery and the Slave Trade System

Every tusk, piece and scrap in the posession of an Arab trader has been steeped and dyed in blood. Every pound weight has cost the life of a man, woman, or child, for every five pounds a hut has been burned, for every two tusks a whole village has been destroyed, every twenty tusks have been obtained at the price of a district with all its people, villages, and plantations. It is simply incredible that, because ivory is required . . . populations, tribes, and nations should be utterly destroyed.

HENRY M. STANLEY, 1895

THE SPANISH AND PORTUGUESE

From about 1415 until his death in 1460, Prince Henry the Navigator, as he was known, was the inspiration for Portuguese explorations. As the slave trade took hold in the soil of the Caribbean plantations, the Portuguese further developed their prowess and mastery of the sea along the Guinea coast of Africa. Wishing to join forces with an ally who would help to counteract the influence of Islam on the African continent, Henry sent out explorers to search for Prester John. This legendary priest-king was believed to be a black Christian monarch who reigned somewhere in Ethiopia or Asia.

According to a twelfth-century legend, the powerful and rich kingdom of Prester John had been cut off from the rest of the Christian world by the spread of Islam. In the fifteenth century and while making their first explorations of the Indian Ocean coasts of Africa, the Portuguese again heard the tale of a Christian king whose kingdom was now believed to be somewhere in the African interior. It was the intent of the Portuguese to proselytize among Prester John's people, convert them to Catholicism, and once an alliance was formed, engage them in the struggle to wrest authority and influence from the Mohammedans. Also, as observed by W.E.B. Du Bois in *The World and Africa,* ''Henry [had] heard of the gold for which the Carthaginians had bartered at Timbuktu.''

The expeditions of the Portuguese continued after Henry's death. It is believed that Christopher Columbus may have been a member of the Portuguese expedition that in 1482 bulilt Elmina Castle, which later became a slave fort. Certainly he was aware of the great profits to be realized from direct sea trade with lands beyond the European continent. While it is not known conclusively that Columbus was employed in the construction of Elmina Castle, in 1482 he did travel to Madeira and the West African Gulf of Guinea in the service of King John II of Portugal.

Ten years later, Columbus offered his services, first to the Portuguese (who rejected his plans) and then to the sovereign heads of Spain. He had conceived the idea that a route to Asia, more direct than the one the Portuguese were seeking by rounding the southern tip of Africa, could be found by sailing directly westward, across the Atlantic Ocean. His proposal included the provision that he be provided

The legendary "Prester John, King of Abyssinia," as he appears on a map of southeastern Africa printed in 1599. (From *Africa on Maps Dating from the Twelfth to the Eighteenth Century . . .* by Egon Klemp.)

A seventeenth-century print of Elmina Castle. This detail comes from a Dutch map of 1658 entitled "Africa Nova Descriptio." (From *Dictionary of African Biography*, vol. 1.)

Christopher Columbus (1446?-1506). With the discovery of the New World came a demand for people to work its plantations—a demand that was met by the institution of slavery. (Courtesy of the Library of Congress, Prints and Photographs Division.)

with three ships by the king, a significant portion of whatever new trade developed, the office of governor over any new lands he might discover, the title of admiral, and a rank in the nobility. These privileges were to be inherited by his son.

By 1477 Portuguese sailors and explorers had already sailed down the west coast of Africa and as far south as the Azores, almost reaching the equator. They were in search of gold, gems, spices, and healing drugs for the European markets—items that could at that time only be obtained by long and costly overland caravans. The success of the Portuguese in sailing around the Cape of Good Hope was due to the invention of the çaravel, a ship that could gain ground against the wind.

Columbus sailed from Spain on August 3, 1492. Following a successful voyage and triumphant return to Spain, he was given the titles of ''Admiral of the Ocean Sea'' and ''Viceroy of the Indies.'' These were more than ceremonial titles, and

The development of the lighter, faster ships known as *caravels* made possible the European exploration and circumnavigation of the African coast. (From *The Growth of African Civilization: West Africa 1000–1800,* by Basil Davidson.)

with the blessing of the Spanish sovereigns he was ordered to organize a second voyage and colonize Hispaniola (the western half of the island of Haiti) while engaged in further exploration of the Caribbean islands. This time, Columbus sailed with a fleet of seventeen vessels.

On his second voyage to the islands of the West Indies, and with the help of slave labor, Columbus attempted to colonize Hispaniola, and there established the first Spanish settlement near the present city of Cap-Haïtien. Here he ruled with his brother Diego. Calling the natives Indians (believing that he had reached the East Indies), Columbus seized the opportunity to rival the Portuguese who had spurned him. First enslaving the indigenous people, he envisioned the new land as a vast center of trade that would enable him to compete with Africa in providing slave labor for the European market.

By 1494 Christopher Columbus had begun the Atlantic slave trade and had introduced the slave-trade system to the New World. For it was on West Indian plantations that the first major demand for this new trade commodity occurred. As for the slaves, Columbus established a quota of gold dust to be produced by each. The slaves were required to wear tags round their necks. Their quotas were recorded every three-months, or when met.

While few historians have mentioned the subject, Columbus's views on slavery are expressed in correspondence and official documents dispatched to Spain. In a letter addressed to the king and queen of Castile and Aragon in April 1493, Columbus observed that " . . . as many slaves as their Highnesses shall command [will] be shipped." In a memorial sent from Santo Domingo, Columbus referred to the native population of Puerto Rico and Santo Domingo as "cannibals," and wrote:

> . . . Seeing how necessary here are cattle and beasts of labor for the maintenance of the people who will be here, and for the good of all these islands, your Highnesses may give license and permission to a sufficient number of caravels to come each year and bring those cattle and other goods and things for settling the country and benefitting from the land, and at the prices reasonable to the costs of those who would bring them, which things can be paid them in slaves from these cannibals, people so rough and willing and well proportioned and of very good understanding, which, taken from that inhumanity, we believe will be better than any other slaves. . . .

The system of slavery that Columbus instituted continued to grow. In 1498, when again the settlers complained of too little gold and poor living conditions, Columbus appeased them by increasing their acreage and permitting the enslavement of Indians to work the land.

At just this time, Europe was entering into a new era of spiritualism and morality. Queen Isabella was becoming sensitive to increased criticisms launched against the Catholic Church and the claim of the Holy Roman Empire to be the supreme secular ruler. She was reluctant to accept Columbus's proposal to enslave the Indians. Believing that the Indians had not been shown "Christian mercy," Queen Isabella countermanded Columbus's order to sell the Indians as slaves. Going further, she decreed that they should be returned to their homes. Subsequently, after years of heated debate, the *Laws of the Indies* (1542) proclaimed the rights of Indians as free men and forbade their enslavement.

While this debate raged, events and developments occurred that had far-reaching effects on the history of Africa. Among them were: the discovery of gold in the West Indies, the discovery of silver in Peru, the growth of Europe's demand for sugar, and the establishment of forts by European powers along some 300 miles of the West Coast of Africa. In 1502, Spanish-born blacks were imported to Hispaniola as slaves. They were the sons and daughters of those first kidnapped Africans who were sold to the Spaniards in the fifteenth century by the Portuguese. It was these blacks who, among themselves and the native Indians, were among the first to offer resistance to chattel slavery. Also of great importance during this era was the stirring of Europe to throw off the yoke of the pope. The beginning of the Protestant Reformation came in 1517, under the leadership of Martin Luther. The Reformation led directly to the establishment of state churches, where in England, for example, it gave rise to a new feeling of nationalism. With the division of Europe between the

Catholic countries of the south and the Protestant countries of the north, the dominance of Portugal and Spain as the most powerful countries in trade and on the high seas began to diminish.

In 1504, Columbus returned to Spain in disgrace. As early as 1494 rumblings had been heard from the early Spanish settlers in the Caribbean. Some, returning to Spain, accused Columbus of cruelty and of being a hard taskmaster. Left to govern while his brother Christopher continued his explorations of the Caribbean Islands, Diego had been unable to maintain discipline and order. Columbus was replaced as governor of Hispaniola. The new governor, Nicolas de Ovando, was joined by Bartolomé de las Casas. Formerly a planter, de las Casas became a Dominican missionary. Shocked and dismayed at the treatment accorded the Indians, it was de las Casas who suggested in 1517 that each new Spanish colonist to the islands be licensed to import a dozen African slaves. With this recommendation, the Atlantic slave-trade system began in earnest.

SLAVERY IN AFRICA AND THE WESTERN HEMISPHERE

The growth of civilizations in the river valleys of Asia and Africa gave rise to the development of organized socio-economic-political systems. As villages, towns, city-states, and empires developed and flourished, workers were needed to meet the demands of larger populations. In the countryside, where family and tribal groups banded together, communal living provided for a more equitable division of labor than in urban settings and trade centers. In the urban areas, systems of government became more complex, and the increased need for labor was met through warfare and conquest. As captives were integrated into the work force, the large city-states soon discovered the value of making slaves of prisoners, thus significantly increasing the production of goods and services while permitting men who had previously been farmers to become full-time soldiers. Further, as the possession of slaves became an indication of wealth and status, the demand for slaves led to rivalries and warfare between neighboring tribes.

As human settlements have developed, almost all civilizations have known some form of slavery. Ancient Egypt, Mesopotamia, Greece, and Rome all had slaves. Varied nomenclatures have described those who were bound into the service of others, and history has recorded the practice of slavery among the ancient Chinese, Africans, and Hebrews.

Admittedly, in ancient times slavery was harsh and oppressive. Yet nothing could equal or rival the dehumanizing process that became an integral part of the Atlantic slave-trade system. A critical factor was the removal of slaves from the African continent and away from the safeguards of a society in which slaves and masters most often were of the same race, culture, and language stock. For in the New World, there was no arbitration between master and slave; there were no family or tribal traditions to be observed; and there was no higher tribunal to appeal to in cases of unfair or unjust treatment. Since most European nations were themselves competing for the monopoly of the lucrative trade in human flesh, there was no cry of indignation from the world community. The Catholic Church sanctioned slavery as the ships, teeming with their black cargoes, were blessed by the pope and high officials of the church as they embarked on their voyages to the Spanish colonies in the Caribbean and the Americas. Moral, social, economic, or political sanctions were not imposed against those who violated every cardinal law and right of human decency as they engaged in the slave trade, called by John Wesley "this execrable sum of all villainies."

By the end of the fifteenth century, the Portuguese were well acquainted with Africa's west coast. In 1482 there appeared the first of many forts that would be built from St. Louis, at the mouth of the Senegal River, to the Gulf of Guinea. Dotting the West African coast for more than 300 miles, the forts bore such names as Axim, Dixcove, Sekondi, Elmina, Cape Coast, Kormantine, and Christianborg.

For a period of nearly two centuries, European interests in West Africa were confined to coastal trading forts and posts from which slaves could be secured for export to America. With the division of the new lands between Spain and Portugal by the pope in 1493, Spain was unable to establish forts on the African continent. She had received most of the New World, and Portugal was granted Brazil, Africa, and most of the land in Asia. Because of this agreement, Spain had to contract with other nations and grant them the right to bring slaves into Spanish colonies. Since Portugal already had a foothold in Africa, she was the first to receive the *asiento* or contract.

As reflected in the race to build forts, from the end of the sixteenth century and until the beginning of the nineteenth, the slave trade was dominated by the Dutch, the French, and the English. The Danes and the Swedes also participated, but on a much smaller scale.

At first the forts were built as fortified storehouses. Water, supplies of fresh food, and firewood were kept there. Some forts were equipped to make minor repairs to ships. However, the main reason for fortifying these trading posts was to maintain the Portuguese trade monopoly and to prevent outside influence.

The Europeans did not have any territorial jurisdiction beyond the walls of their forts; yet this foothold, alone, was enough to permit the extending of their sphere of influence into the neighboring villages, townships, and kingdoms. This influence would leave an indelible scar on the character of the African continent, with long and devastating consequences. The occupied land was rented or leased. With the establishment of a permanent trading post, each of the European nations attempted to control the trade by negotiating exclusive trading rights with local rulers and chieftains.

Between the fifteenth and nineteenth centuries, there were three distinct periods of fort building. Lasting for almost 130 years, the first period occurred in the sixteenth century and was dominated by the Portuguese. The second period saw the brief ascendance of the Dutch between 1637-1642. (The Dutch, however, would never receive an exclusive right to trade.) The third period of fort-building began with the initiative taken by Henry Caerlof. A former employee of the Dutch West India Company, Caerlof had shown the English how to build their first fort at Kormantine in 1631. The chain of forts built by Caerlof was actually financed by the Dutch. Once constructed, however, the forts were then leased to other sovereign governments. The Swedes occupied one of them in 1649. Remaining until 1656, they were followed by the Danes. Still on the Guinea Coast as late as 1670, Caerlof was retained by the French to superintend the building of forts on the Slave Coast at the Bight of Benin.

Because of the rivalry and competition for trade along the Gold Coast, many forts in this region were built in close proximity to each other. Some were only a scant mile apart. The slave ships would anchor nearby, awaiting slaves to fill their holds.

During these centuries the African slave trade flourished and, like many others, Bornu became a supplier of the black gold that flowed across the trans-Saharan trade routes. In exchange for its chief export of slaves, Bornu received its main import of horses.

Women, too, were a part of the slave coffles that trekked their way to Africa's West Coast and unknown lands. Their lamenting wails and plaintive cries told the story of their sorrow and desperation. One such song, recorded in the 1840s by the abolitionists, was published by John Greenleaf Whittier. Symbolically, the Bornu women sang of "Rubee," or gold, and of "Arka," their freedom papers. This song—and others like it—was preserved and transported across the Atlantic during the dreaded "Middle Passage" from the African homeland to a Caribbean seasoning plantation, then on to America, in the hold of a slave ship.

Song of the Bornu Slaves

Where are we going? Where are we going?
Where are we going, Rubee?
Hear us, save us, make us free,
Send our Arka down from thee!
Here the Ghiblee wind is blowing,
Strange and large the world is growing!
Tell us, Rubee, where are we going?
Where are we going, Rubee?

Bornu! Bornu! Where is Bornu!
Where are we going, Rubee?
Bornu-land was rich and good,
Wells of water, fields of food;
Bornu-land we see no longer,
Here we thirst, and here we hunger,
Here the Moor man smites in anger;
Where are we going, Rubee?

Where are we going? Where are we going?
Hear us, save us, Rubee!
Moons of marches from our eyes,
Bornu-land behind us lies;
Hot the desert wind is blowing,
Wild the waves of sand are flowing!
Hear us! tell us, Where are we going?
Where are we going, Rubee?

Slaves being rowed to ships waiting off the coast of Africa. (Courtesy of Harvard University, Peabody Museum.)

None escaped the horrors of the Middle Passage, in which crew and captives alike were reduced to a brutish state, exposed to disease and death. The cruelty and inhumanity of the trade were described in a report to the British House of Commons:

> The Negroes were chained to each other hand and foot, and stowed so close that they were not allowed above a foot and a half for each in breadth. Thus rammed . . . like herring in a barrel, they contracted . . . fatal disorders; so that they who came to inspect them in the morning had . . . to pick up dead slaves out of their rows, and to unchain . . . [them] from the bodies of their wretched fellow-sufferers. . . .

The total disregard for human life becomes abundantly clear when it is understood that every hazard and risk associated with the trade was a calculated one. For every piece of cargo or merchandise that was exported in the conduct of the triangular trade was heavily insured.

Directly related to the success of the trade were a number of economic variables that significantly contributed to the law of supply and demand. Thousands died from the effects of ''seasoning.'' Other factors had to be considered. One was the declining birth rate among slave women of childbearing age; another was the cost and advantage of raising a slave over and above the cost of importing an adult slave who could be purchased on long-term credit. Most slave owners found it cheaper to import slaves than to breed them, thus creating an ever-growing market for captured Africans.

By the 1780s it was estimated that the average number of slaves being taken each year from the West African coast had reached 93,000. Many were now being exported to the American colonies from Senegambia, the Sierre Leone region, the Grain and Ivory coasts, the Slave Coast, and the Niger Delta and Cameroon areas, as well as other parts of the continent.

As America approached the threshold of the Revolution, many considered the paradox of wanting freedom for themselves while holding others in bondage. On March 23, 1775, Patrick Henry, speaking before the Virginia Provincial Convention, concluded a stirring address with the following sentiments: "Is life so dear, or peace so sweet, as to be purchased at the price of chains and slavery? . . . I know not what course others may take, but as for me, give me liberty, or give me death!" While the speech was not intended to be an antislavery address, it does reflect the thinking of the time concerning "natural rights"—rights that were violated for millions of Africans.

On June 11, 1776, Thomas Jefferson was appointed to serve on the committee to draft the Declaration of Independence. A complex man, Jefferson himself owned slaves. While many called him an egalitarian, Jefferson was an embodiment of his age's mixed reactions to slavery and the presence of blacks in America. In his original draft of the Declaration of Independence, Jefferson charged the king of England with "wag[ing] a cruel war against human nature itself, violating its most sacred rights of life and liberty in the persons of a distant people who never offended him, capturing and carrying them into slavery in another hemisphere, or to incur miserable death in their transportation thither. . . ."

Nonetheless, in his *Notes on Virginia,* Thomas Jefferson gave voice to his belief that the black mental capacity was inferior to that of whites. This brought a sharp retort from the Afro-American astronomer and mathematician Benjamin Banneker, who sent Jefferson—then secretary of state—a copy of the almanac he had published in the 1790s. In the accompanying letter, he wrote:

. . . I freely and cheerfully acknowledge, that I am of the African race, and in that color which is natural to them of the deepest dye; and it is under a sense of the most profound gratitude to the Supreme Ruler of the Universe . . . that I am not under that tyrannical thraldom, and inhuman captivity, to which too many of my brethren are doomed, . . . that I have abundantly tasted of the fruition of those blessings, which proceed from that free and unequalled liberty with which you are favored. . . .

In conclusion, to inform Jefferson that the almanac had been published (and to dispel the myth of mental inferiority), Banneker noted: " . . . I choose to send it [the almanac] to you in manuscript . . . that . . . you might also view it in my own handwriting."

The Declaration of Independence was adopted by the Congress on July 4, 1776. The indictment against the king of England was deleted to appease the Southern members of the drafting committee who were slaveholders and the Northern members who were slave traders and rum merchants. The thought of giving slaves "inalienable rights" was unconscionable for most of the nation.

Many years later, the former slave Frederick Douglass would ask the stinging rhetorical question: "What to the American slave is your fourth of July?"

III. LET YOUR MOTTO BE RESISTANCE
Slave Revolts in the Caribbean and the United States

The spectacular and astonishing triumph of revolution in Haiti threatened the whole slave system of the West Indies and even of continental America. It was this revolt more than any other single thing that spelled [the] doom not only of the African slave trade but of slavery in America as a basis of an industrial system.

W.E.B. Du Bois
The World and Africa

PRELUDE TO REBELLION

By the middle of the eighteenth century there were few manufacturing towns in England that had not realized great profits from the triangular Atlantic slave trade. Procured through the use of slave labor in the sugar-producing plantations of the Caribbean, these profits were one of the main financial sources of the Industrial Revolution.

During this period of the history of chattel slavery, a smaller triangular trade developed and operated within the larger triangle. Sloops and vessels built in New England and commissioned in such port cities as Providence, Rhode Island, sailed south to Barbados, then north to Charleston, South Carolina, and returned to the New England coastal states. Their cargo was rum, used to purchase slaves and molasses. The slaves were taken off the boats along the route from Charleston to Providence and sold in lots to dealers and to individual buyers. The molasses was used to produce more rum.

Soon after 1800, Southern port towns and cities began to discourage the importation of Caribbean slaves, believing them rebellious and troublesome. Despite the constitutional provision that provided for the abolition of the foreign trade by January 1, 1808, the Southern states began a direct commerce with the African continent.

Just as American slave dealers began to establish contact with the West Coast of Africa and realize profits from the trade, the demand in England and America for the suppression of the African slave trade was on the rise. American slave traders were angered that their participation in the trade (which was the basis for their agricultural economic system) was being threatened. Condemned because of constitutional questions and moral convictions, Southern slaveholders rebuked those who, themselves, had reaped great profits from slavery and would now deny them the same opportunity. As stated by W.E.B. Du Bois in *The World and Africa:*

> . . . [England] proved the only land able to raise wages and yet maintain high profit[s] by shifting the burden of pauperized toil to the colonies and dominated peoples, and at the same time, although author and chief supporter of modern

slavery, . . . could hold up her head and, by suppressing a [system of] slavery now becoming unprofitable, lead world philanthropy as the great emancipator of the slave.

Before we can understand the development of chattel slavery in America and the Caribbean and the resistance it inspired, we must understand earlier economic systems. In particular, we must briefly review the European class struggle of laboring and subjugated peoples.

In western Europe, feudalism was a political and military system, providing a structure for government and defense. During the Middle Ages, as feudalism spread from northern Europe into England and southern Europe, it did not include an economic system. This dimension was added during the eighth century when Moslems from Africa began their migration into Europe through Spain. Subjugated, many became serfs under feudal lords, whose ranks were filled only with aristocrats and those of noble birth. Bound to the soil, the serfs enjoyed a status somewhere between that of free men and slaves. While historians of the medieval period make a distinction between feudalism and manoralism, both systems severely abridged the freedoms of the laboring class.

An economic system that did not last very long, manoralism began in Europe during the Middle Ages and lasted only until about 1200. It gave rise to a large peasant class that became the tillers of the soil. Considered the property of the manoral lords and included in their real estate, these peasants were bound to the land and required to produce for themselves and their masters. Unlike chattel slaves, they could not be sold apart from the land.

These political-military-economic systems continued until the rise of towns, the establishment of centralized governments, the invention of gunpowder and other sophisticated weapons of warfare, and the revitalization of an economic system that employed currency in the payment of wages for goods and services. Declining first in western Europe, these systems continued in some regions of central and eastern Europe until the beginning of the nineteenth century.

But the decline of feudalism, manoralism, and serfdom was not a peaceful evolution. Rather, industrialization and progress came as a direct result of the revolts initiated by serfs. Escaping to towns and cities and demanding payment for their labor, in time the serfs gained their freedom. By the seventeenth century, English law recognized their right to freedom and liberty. Growing out of guilds and the domestic system (in which entire families of former serfs were engaged in the production of goods for English and European markets), the Industrial Revolution was financed in part by profits realized from forced slave labor in the Caribbean and in the American colonies.

Chattel slavery was first and foremost an economic system. From this perspective, slave revolts in the Caribbean islands and American colonies can be seen as a continuation of the class struggle among laborers in bondage. As noted by W.E.B. Du Bois in *The World and Africa:* ''The slave revolts were the beginnings of the revolutionary struggle for the uplift of the laboring masses in the modern world.''

In the Caribbean, the most determined revolutionary group was the Maroons, who were descendants of escaped African slaves in the West Indies. The Maroons were organized under chiefs. Among them were Père Jean, 1697; Michel, 1713; Colas, 1720; Polydor, 1730; the legendary Macandel[4], 1758; Canga, 1777; and Santiague, 1782. One of their greatest leaders was Jean-François, who was succeeded by Biassou; Toussaint L'Ouverture followed Biassou.

Toussaint L'Ouverture finally achieved the Maroons' goal of a free Haiti; but the struggle for that freedom was long and hard. The following brief chronology[5] shows the growth of the Spanish, French, and English influences in the Caribbean and West Africa. It traces some of the most important developments and events in the bloody history of the struggle for Haitian independence and takes us up to the rise to power of Toussaint L'Ouverture.

1625	The French take possession of Haiti.
1626	The establishment of St. Louis, the first settlement on the Senegal River.
1642–1645	The French import African slaves to the island of Martinique.
1650	Sugar planting begins in Martinique. Within a century 60,000 slaves will populate the island. Three revolts and a civil war will be necessary to free them.
1679	Haitian slaves revolt.
1684	The expansion of sugar and tobacco growing in the Caribbean. Great Britain begins to rival France and Spain for dominion in the West Indies.
1691	Haitian slaves revolt.
1701	The French develop a system of slavery that will have far-reaching consequences upon the world's economic system.
1779	Eight hundred black Haitian volunteers fight with the Americans in the Revolutionary War.
1780	The French enter into a treaty with the Maroons in Santo Domingo.
1788	29,500 slaves are imported to Santo Domingo. Transported in 98 vessels, 15,000 are men, 7,000 are women, 7,500 are children.
1790	Vincent Ogé[6] leads a slave insurrection in Santo Domingo.

---

[4]The black prophet Macandel was born in Guinea. After losing a hand on a Caribbean plantation, Macandel became a herdsman and was assigned to guarding cattle. About 1751 he escaped into the mountainous regions of Haiti. Rising to leadership among the Maroons, he organized them into a force to wage guerrilla warfare and free blacks from white domination. In 1758 he was betrayed. Accused of being a "seducer, profaner, and poisoner," he met death at the stake.

[5]Selected dates from Irene Diggs, *Chronology of Notable Events and Dates in the History of the African and His Descendants During the Period of Slavery and the Slave Trade.*

[6]Vincent Ogé was a Parisian mulatto whose mother owned a plantation in Santo Domingo. Favoring abolition, he planned to return to Haiti and help mulattoes gain their full civil rights. His intentions became known and the French authorities refused to allow him to embark for Santo Domingo from a French port. Therefore, he went to England (where he was aided by abolitionist Thomas Clarkson) and sailed to Charleston, South Carolina. From there he reached his mother's plantation in Haiti. Ogé led some 300 recruits into battle, but was outnumbered by 1,500 men with artillery. He then fled to Spanish territory, but was handed over to the French who sentenced him to be broken on the wheel.

| 1794 | Toussaint L'Ouverture raises flag of the Republic of Haiti; deserts the Spanish and joins the French with his troops. |
| 1798 | October 1, Toussaint enters Mole St. Nicholas as conqueror. He signs a treaty with England that recognizes his sovereignty and Haiti's independence, and enters into commercial agreements. |

TOUSSAINT L'OUVERTURE AND THE CARIBBEAN

You think you have rooted up the tree of liberty, but I am only a branch; I have planted the tree so deep that all France can never root it up.

Toussaint L'Ouverture

In May 1799, the commander-in-chief of the British expeditionary force to Santo Domingo was warned that the island of Jamaica and the United States mainland were in danger of an attack by armed forces. These forces were, in the words of C. L. R. James in *A History of Pan-African Revolt,* part of "the only successful Negro revolt, the only successful slave revolt in history, [which] had its roots in the French Revolution. . . . [With] the slogans of liberty, equality and fraternity, the political excitement . . . awoke the sleeping slaves to revolution." Made up of an army of some 55,000 men, the rumored invasion was to be led by Toussaint L'Ouverture.

Toussaint L'Ouverture was one of the most remarkable men of his time. Under his able leadership and skillful administration, the slaves of Haiti were liberated. Further, Toussaint forced Napoleon to abandon his dream of an American empire and sell the vast Louisiana Territory to the Americans. Even though opposed to trading with the new black republic, Thomas Jefferson felt that the American government had to recognize the independence of Haiti.

Toussaint L'Ouverture proved to be a formidable opponent. The son of slave parents, he was born about 1774, possibly on November 1, a day celebrated by the French as All Saint's Day (Fête de Toussaint). Christened François Dominique Toussaint and the eldest of eight children, he was a devout Catholic. Like other slaves, he was known by his master's surname, Breda. As a young slave he was allowed to read, and it was probably the French author Abbé Raynal who first awakened him to the ideas of freedom and liberty and raised the poignant question: "What should be done to overthrow slavery?" The following passage from Raynal's work is typical of the revolutionary ideas that were sweeping the Western world at the time.

Self-interest alone governs kings and nations; a courageous chief is all the Negroes need: where is he? Where is the great man whom nature owes to her vexed, oppressed and tormented children? He will doubtless appear; he will come forth and raise the sacred standard of liberty. This venerable signal will gather around him his companions in misfortune. More impetuous than the torrents, they will elsewhere leave the indelible trace of their just resentment. Everywhere people will bless the name of the hero who shall have re-established the rights of the human race.

Toussaint L'Ouverture, Haitian liberator. (Charcoal drawing by Lois Mailou Jones. Reproduction courtesy of Louise Daniel Hutchinson.)

At the end of the eighteenth century, Santo Domingo's population included 30,000 whites, 20,000 free mulattoes, and 500,000 black slaves. The white population, greatly encouraged by the success of the American colonies in gaining their independence from England, wanted to declare their independence from France. The mulattoes, who enjoyed the status of their white slave-master fathers and were able to own property and share in inheritances, wanted to achieve full political and civil rights. Spurned by the whites and the mulattoes, on August 22, 1791, the slaves once again began to revolt, hoping to gain and defend their freedom.

When the planters learned that some four thousand slaves had arisen, they requested help from English troops stationed in Jamaica. The rebelling slaves sought asylum with the Spanish on the eastern portion of the island (Haiti). This was the situation when Toussaint L'Ouverture emerged to join and lead the black soldiers. At the time he rose to this position of power and influence, Toussaint had been a slave for forty-seven years, and the spirit of liberty had been ignited in Haiti.

In his *Speeches, Lectures, and Letters,* Wendell Phillips provides us with an interesting analysis of Toussaint L'Ouverture's accomplishments. Comparing Toussaint's military career with that of Cromwell and Napoleon, Phillips writes:

. . . This man never saw a soldier until he was fifty. . . . This man manufactured his army out of what? Out of what you call the despicable race of negroes [sic], debased, demoralized by two hundred years of slavery, one hundred thousand of them imported into the island within four years, unable to speak a dialect intelligible even to each other. Yet out of this mixed, and as you say, despicable mass, he forged a thunderbolt and hurled it at what? At the proudest blood in Europe, the Spaniard, and sent him home conquered; at the most warlike blood in Europe, the French, and put him under his feet; at the pluckiest blood in Europe, the English, and they skulked home to Jamaica. . . . The soldiers were proud of their general and under his guidance performed miracles. . . .

Clearing the island of all foreign enemies, Toussaint L'Ouverture restored peace and prosperity. Believing that he could ameliorate differences and establish friendship between the slaves and their former masters, Toussaint presented a five-year work agreement that enabled the former masters to receive one-fourth of their own production with assessments for their subsistence. He opened all Haitian ports and became the first ruler in the world to establish a policy of free trade.

Betrayed by Napoleon, the brief peace was soon shattered. In January 1802 the French fleet sailed to carry out Napoleon's decree of May 1801, to crush Toussaint and restore slavery in Haiti. The threat of reenslavement was a ploy to assure Toussaint's entrapment. In response to the threat, Toussaint declared he would order the capital city burned, vowing to continue the fight over its ashes.

In 1802 Toussaint L'Ouverture was betrayed by some of his generals. Captured and marched through the streets of his city in chains, Toussaint was then deported to France and imprisoned near the border of Switerzerland. Here he died in April 1803.

The spirit of liberty and freedom did not die, though. Just six months after Toussaint's death, Rochambeau[7] surrendered. The French were stripped of power in the Caribbean, and Haitian independence was restored.

Continuing his thoughts on Toussaint L'Ouverture, Wendell Phillips writes:

. . . I would call him Napoleon, but Napoleon made his way to empire over broken oaths and a sea of blood. This man never broke his word. "NO RETALIATION" was his great motto and the rule of his life. . . . I would call him Cromwell, but Cromwell was only a soldier, and the state he founded went down with him into his grave. I would call him Washington, but the great Virginian held slaves. This man risked his empire rather than permit the slave trade in the humblest villages of his dominions. You think me fanatic . . . , for you read history, not with your eyes, but with your prejudices. But fifty years hence, when

---

[7]Jean-Baptiste Rochambeau (1725-1807). General marshal of France, 1791-1807; commander of the French army in the American Revolution.

Liberté.   Égalité.

Au fort Liberté ———— le 26. Brumaire
l'an dix de la République française, une et indivisible.
(17. 9bre 1801.)

TOUSSAINT LOUVERTURE,

Gouverneur de Saint-Domingue,

à Monsieur Tobias Lear Agent général
des Etats unis à St. Domingue au Cap ————

Monsieur

Je vous invite à encourager vos Concitoyens à
faire des Expéditions pour ce port; le tribunal,
et les autorités y sont déjà installées; le port
est un des plus beaux, et des plus sûrs de Saint
Domingue; et par les mesures que je viens de
prendre les Denrées y seront très abondantes;
j'ai lieu d'espérer que vous ferez tout ce qui
dépendra de vous pour encourager vos compatriotes
à le fréquenter.
J'ai l'honneur d'être avec la plus parfaite
Considération.
Monsieur ————   Votre très humble, et très
                      obéissant serviteur

Letter dated "26 Brumaire" (September 17, 1801) from Toussaint L'Ouverture to Tobias Lear, the United States general agent to Santo Domingo, asking him to encourage trade between the two nations. (Courtesy of the Connecticut Historical Society.)

Truth gets a hearing, the Muse of History will put Phocion[8] for the Greeks, Brutus[9] for the Romans, Hampden[10] for England, Fayette[11] for France, choose Washington as the brightest . . . of our earlier civilizations, and John Brown as the ripe fruit of our noon-day; then, dipping her pen in the sunlight, will write in the clear blue, above them all, the name of the soldier, the statesman, the martyr, TOUSSAINT L'OUVERTURE.

RESISTANCE IN THE UNITED STATES

The year 1800 was a pivotal one in American history. In this year John Brown and Nat Turner were born, Denmark Vesey purchased his freedom, and Gabriel Prosser was hanged for plotting a slave insurrection. Having won its independence from Great Britain, by the end of 1800 a new, united, and centralized government was rising on the banks of the Potomac River. As President John Adams and the townspeople of the newly created federal city greeted the barges bringing the belongings of the Continental Congress, no one could foresee the events that were so soon to follow. In particular, the Louisiana Purchase in 1803 and the War of 1812 would have lasting effects on the chattel system of slavery and the Atlantic slave trade.

Before telling of the response and resistance to the brutalizing experience of slavery by the African slaves and their descendants, it is important to review some of the events that directly led to revolts, insurrections, and unrest in nineteenth-century America. Among these events were:

1617 The founding and development of the Dutch West India Company.
1619 The arrival of the first Africans into the Virginia Colony.
1621 The Dutch West India Company is given the monopoly of the slave trade.
1662 Passage of the Virginia law declaring that children should either be held in bondage or declared free according to the status of the mother.
1663 What may have been the first serious conspiracy involving African slaves in English American colonies occurs in Virginia.
1672 Fugitive slaves in Virginia attempt to form small armed groups.
1680 Passage of law in New York colony that restricts the meeting of four or more slaves away from their master's service and prohibits possession or carrying of arms.
1687 Slave conspiracy to revolt in Virginia.
1692 Passage of act in Virginia providing that "resisting" or runaway slaves may

---

[8]Phocion (402?-317B.C.). Athenian statesman and general.

[9]Marcus Junius Brutus (85?-42 B.C.). Roman provincial administrator; one of the assassins of Julius Caesar, emperor of Rome.

[10]John Hampden (1594-1643). British statesman who defended the rights of the House of Commons against Charles I.

[11]Fayette (or LaFayette, 1757-1834). French soldier, statesman, and liberal leader, who served in the American Revolutionary Army and took a leading part in the French Revolution in 1789 and the revolution of 1830.

be lawfully killed and the master reimbursed 4,000 pounds of tobacco from public funds for the loss of the slave.

1712 New York and Massachusetts enact laws to prevent, suppress, and punish the conspiracy and insurrection of Africans and other slaves.

1720 Slave conspiracy in South Carolina.

1722 Slaves plot to revolt in Virginia.

1724 Black code with fifty-five articles governing the actions of slaves is published in New Orleans.

1739 Slave insurrection at Stono, South Carolina.

1749 First importation of African slaves into Georgia colony.

1750 Passage of British act to extend and improve the African slave trade.

1750 Due to revolts and threats of unrest, Parliament declares that for every four slaves in the Georgia colony there should be at least one white male servant of age to bear arms. Africans are to be employed only in agriculture; slaves to be apprenticed only to carpenters and not taught any other trade.

1761 Complaint to the British Crown that slaves in South Carolina have begun again the "hellish practice of poisoning."

1774 African slaves in Boston conspire to strike for liberty and seek aid from the British.

1785 Birth of David Walker, who in 1829 publishes his famous *Appeal* advocating slave uprisings as the only possible solution to the plight of the American slave.

1787 Founding of the Philadelphia Free African Society.

1788 Protest under the leadership of the African Prince Hall against the kidnapping and sale of free blacks into slavery.

1800 Gabriel Prosser's revolt near Richmond, Virginia.

Even this brief outline gives an idea of how troubled and complex were the relations between black and white America at the time of the Louisiana Purchase. The buying of this land in 1803 significantly altered the history of the United States and was connected with the revolutionary developments in Haiti.

With approximately one-half of the North American continent in the possession of France and Spain, Thomas Jefferson, then president, was afraid that the French and Spanish, as allies, threatened the sovereignty of the American states. With the redeclaration of Haitian independence, the influence of France as a colonial power was on the decline. To protect the westernmost borders of the United States, Jefferson proposed joining with England to wage an Anglo-American war against France. Having lost Haiti and finding himself confronted with this possible alliance, Napoleon agreed to the sale of the Louisiana Territory, and on May 2, 1803, the treaty for purchase was signed. With the loss of Haiti and the Louisiana Territory, Napoleon abandoned his dream of building an empire in the Western Hemisphere.

At a cost of $15 million, the acquisition of 827,987 square miles doubled the size of the country. From east to west, this vast area lay between the Mississippi River and the Rocky Mountains; from north to south, it stretched from Canada to the Gulf of Mexico.

The purchase of the Louisiana Territory encouraged the expansion of slavery and the slave-trade system. Earlier, Spain had introduced sugar cane into this region, and the new land provided for the growth of the cotton economy. A slave labor force was needed to produce both of these cash crops.

Even though there was a fear of slave insurrections, in 1803 South Carolina reopened her ports to the African slave trade in order to meet the new demand for a labor force. The following year an effort was made to have Congress pass a resolution banning the importation of slaves into the new territory. In his State of the Union message in 1806, Jefferson reminded the legislators of their constitutional duty to end the importation of slaves from foreign lands by January 1, 1808. Further, he counseled that appropriate measures be taken to cease expeditions to Africa that could not be completed by that date. But to the embarrassment of England (now an ally of the United States), which censured other nations for their continued involvement in the trade, the Americans escalated their trafficking in slaves.

While these events were taking place, the slave population was not oblivious to the spirit of liberty and nationalism that had been awakened during the American Revolution; neither was it unmindful of Jeffersonian Republicanism and the era of the common man. Although slaves were only on the periphery of this new movement, it served as a catalyst for their own desire to achieve freedom.

Beginning with Gabriel Prosser's revolt in 1800, the first decades of the nineteenth century were marked by responses and resistance to slavery that took many forms. These manifested themselves in both overt and clandestine activities.

A slave auction in Virginia. (Courtesy of The New-York Historical Society.)

The significance of these acts of resistance is not to be determined by their success or failure, but rather by the fact that so many did make the commitment to seek and defend their freedom.

By 1810 the unrest among slaves and the desire for freedom had crossed the Allegheny Mountains, and slaves in Lexington, Kentucky, were conspiring to revolt. The following year, slaves only recently transported into the region revolted in Louisiana. In 1829 slave revolts were again reported in Louisiana, and as late as 1862 some Louisiana slaves were demanding wages for their labor.

While Denmark Vesey's planned insurrection (1822), Nat Turner's revolt (1831), and John Brown's raid (1859) are among the better known plans to engage slaves in open rebellion against the "peculiar institution," many free blacks in the northeastern states also organized and developed strategies for resistance in concert with actions taken by their brothers in bondage. Some, like David Walker, took individual initiatives. Published in 1829, *Walker's Appeal*[12] was one of the most inflammatory tracts of its day. Walker, who advocated revolt as the only means to end slavery, died mysteriously in 1830.

On Sunday, August 22, 1831, the slave preacher for a black congregation in Southampton, Virginia, directed its attention to a passage in scripture: "8th Chapter of Revelations and 10th Verse; and he recommended that the whole Chapter should be read before they commenced the Text."[13] The following passage is an example of the clever use of spirituals and scripture as a form of communication among slaves and free blacks.

> . . . And the third angel sounded,
> and there fell from heaven a
> great star, burning like a torch,
> and it fell upon the third part
> of the rivers, and upon the
> fountains of water. . . .

Such biblical passages stirred many blacks, including Nat Turner, a deeply religious man who believed that the prophecy must be fulfilled. Under the cover of darkness on August 22, 1831, he led a revolt in Southampton, Virginia, that left an indelible mark on the history of America and gripped the South with fear. Fifty-five whites were murdered, and between September 5 and 20, 1831, twenty-one blacks were condemned and executed in Southampton. Of this number, slaves Jack and Andrew, the property of Coby Whitehead, were removed to Richmond. Presumably, their punishment was banishment or transportation from the state. Slave Isaac, the property of George H. Charlson(?), was "recommended to mercy."[14] Evading

---

[12]Full title: *Walker's Appeal, in Four Articles: Together with a Preamble, to the Coloured Citizens of the World, but in particular, and very expressly, to those of the United States of America, written in Boston, State of Massachusetts, September 28, 1829.*

[13]Headnote on *List of Whites Murdered by Blacks (1831)*. Manuscript Collection, The College of William and Mary.

[14]*List of Slaves Condemned and Executed at Southampton, Virginia 1831.* Manuscript Collection, The College of William and Mary.

Six weeks after his revolt, Nat Turner was captured in the Dismal Swamp. He was then tried, condemned, and hanged. (Courtesy of the Library of Congress, Prints and Photographs Division.)

his captors and hiding in the swamps for about two months, Turner was finally captured, tried, and hanged in October 1831.

But the will to resist did not die on the gallows with Turner. The very real fear of continued unrest among the slave population (now totaling four million) is reflected in the very stringent slave and black codes enacted by Southern state legislatures.

At this time, a distinction was being made between white and black rebels. The Southern press was very laudatory in its praise of the "noble sons of Poland" who opposed the oppression of the czar. And when revolutions erupted in Latin America and Europe, the South joined the rest of America in encouraging the fighters for liberty. Yet in late August, with receipt of the news of the revolt at Southampton, black rebels were described as "banditti, blood-thirsty wolves and deluded wretches."

Most of white America could not support the efforts of blacks to be free. Even so, the desire for freedom persisted among the black population. As reflected in the documents that follow (see pages 130–148), the will to revolt adds a new dimension of heroic proportion to the character of the American slave, who, in the words of Henry Highland Garnet, let his motto be RESISTANCE!

IV. THE RETURN TO THE SOURCE
The Antislavery, Abolitionist, and Colonization Movements

ABOLITION AND COLONIAL AMERICA

The period from about the mid-eighteenth century to the mid-nineteenth century was one of revolutionary ideas. No longer satisfied to leave government in the hands of noblemen and aristocrats, citizens demanded a part in the decision-making process. In the spirit of revolution, the laboring class continued its struggle against the landed nobility, and the African slave continued to resist perpetual bondage. Collectively, these efforts gave rise to revolutionary thoughts that manifested themselves in three historically significant efforts, namely, the antislavery, abolitionist, and colonization movements. To varying degrees, all considered the proposition of emancipating the slaves and returning some Africans and their Afro-American descendants to the West Coast of Africa.

John Woolman was one of the most important opponents of slavery in colonial America. Like Anthony Benezet in Philadelphia, Woolman believed that the practice of slave-keeping was inconsistent with Christianity. Both men wrote influential antislavery tracts before the Revolutionary War and both were Quakers. Of Benezet it has been said that with a singleness of purpose he worked to make the Quakers and Philadelphians into an effective body of antislavery advocates. In 1759, he founded a school for black and Indian children. The school was later endowed by a provision of his will. Abolitionists Richard Allen and Absalom Jones were among the Philadelphia blacks who came under the influence of Benezet's humanitarian and educational philosophy.

Richard Allen and Absalom Jones were not the only ones to be affected by the work and writings of Anthony Benezet. The English abolitionist Thomas Clarkson thought that Benezet's antislavery pamphlets should be circulated in the British schools "so that rising youth might acquire a . . . detestation of this cruel traffic."

Benjamin Franklin was so moved by the writings of Benezet and John Woolman[15] that even before the Revolutionary War he abandoned the practice of keeping slaves. Another expression of Franklin's concern for blacks was his visit to the

---

[15]In 1762, Benjamin Franklin printed Woolman's antislavery tract *Considerations on Keeping Negroes: Recommended to the Professors of Christianity of every Denomination.*

The Reverend Richard Allen (1760-1831), the first bishop of the African Methodist Episcopal Church, and Absalom Jones were fellow activists in the antislavery cause and organized the Free African Society in Philadelphia in 1787. (Courtesy of Howard University Museum, Moorland-Spingarn Research Center.)

American slave poetess Phillis Wheatley during her stay in London in 1773. By 1785 he was the elected president of the Pennsylvania Society for Promoting the Abolition of Slavery and the Relief of Free Negroes Unlawfully Held in Bondage. Franklin's last public act was his signing of the Society's memorial that was presented to the first Congress on February 12, 1790, requesting the legislators "to countenance the restoration of liberty to unhappy men, who alone, in this land of freedom are degraded into perpetual bondage."

With the conclusion of the Revolutionary War and the adoption of the Declaration of Independence, antislavery sentiment mounted rapidly in the North. This was especially true among the free black population, whose numbers had significantly increased as some 5,000 black soldiers were mustered out of the Continental Army. As Benjamin Quarles in *The Negro in the American Revolution* says: "To the slave soldier, who had borne the responsibilities of citizenship before he could enjoy its rights, it brought freedom and in some instances a land bounty."

While it is most frequently assumed that blacks who served with either the American or the British did receive their freedom at the conclusion of the war, there were exceptions. One was William Lee. Lee had served as Washington's personal body servant during the Revolutionary War. At the war's end, he returned to Mount Vernon and continued in the service of the Washington household staff.

Later, Lee was away from Mount Vernon and in the Philadelphia area for an indefinite period of time. The set of circumstances surrounding his temporary removal from the Washington estate remains obscure, but in 1789 his return was being arranged.

At this time, George Washington's correspondence was carried on by Tobias Lear, his personal secretary. Writing on behalf of Washington, in a letter dated May 3, 1789, Lear requested assistance in arranging for William Lee's return to Mount Vernon. In part, he said: " . . . if he should [be] incline[d] to return . . . you will be so kind as to have him sent in the first vessel that sails to Alexandria . . . altho' he will be troublesome. He has been an old and faithful Servant [and] this is enough for the President to gratify him in every reasonable wish." Now aged and infirm, Lee returned to Mount Vernon in June 1789. In later correspondence, Washington described Lee as able to powder gentlemen's wigs but "scarcely fit for anything else."

Fifteen years later, in 1804, the artist Charles Wilson Peale visited Mount Vernon. There he found William Lee. Although he had been given his freedom when George Washington died in 1799, Lee, now crippled, was in an outbuilding of Washington's estate, cobbling shoes.

ENGLAND AND THE COLONIZATION MOVEMENT

For blacks the gaining of freedom was *the* priority, and for some it did not matter on which side of the Revolutionary War they fought, so long as they gained their liberty. In 1779, many blacks responded to the proclamation issued by British Commander-in-Chief Sir Henry Clinton, offering freedom to those who would join the British army. One who did was African-born Thomas Peters.

In 1776, Thomas Peters declared his own independence and became a fugitive slave. After fleeing to Canada, he joined the British. The inducements were freedom and the promise of land for farming. Peters served in the black arms-bearing Regiment of Guides and Pioneers, and rose to the rank of sergeant. At the end of the war, Peters and his wife settled among Canadian-born blacks in the province of Annapolis Royal in Nova Scotia.

After six years, land had not yet been surveyed; therefore, it could not be developed. Other sites were overgrown with hard-to-clear trees and were otherwise unsuitable for farming. It was these conditions and other grievances that Peters reported to Granville Sharp when he sailed to England in 1791.

In England, Peters hoped to find a sympathetic audience. The first effective move against the slave trade had been initiated by the British Parliament in 1776. A decade later, a proposal was drafted that recommended the founding of a settlement for West Indian and American slaves who had sought refuge in England. This settlement became Sierra Leone. In 1787, a committee for the abolition of slavery was organized in Great Britain. Granville Sharp was its first president. After sixteen years of often heated and lengthy debate, the majority of the British Parliament finally acquiesced and voted with the abolitionist minority. In 1807, England banned the slave trade.

It was into this historical climate that Thomas Peters stepped in 1791. Representing more than two hundred families from the Canadian provinces of Annapolis Royal and New Brunswick, with the help of English abolitionists a memorial was prepared. Signed by Peters—who made his mark—it was presented to the secretary of state for foreign affairs. Declaring their dissatisfaction with conditions in Nova Scotia, the memorialists were prepared to relocate, should a better offer be made.

Following an investigation of the matter, and upon the recommendation of the directors of the newly formed Sierra Leone Company (a group that included Sharp, Wilberforce, and Clarkson), it was decided to relocate the settlers represented by Thomas Peters. At the expense of Great Britain, 1,190 emigrants sailed from Nova

Granville Sharp (1735-1813), an abolitionist in England, where concern for the free black population led to the creation of the Society for the Abolition of the Slave Trade. The Society was founded by Thomas Clarkson, Granville Sharp, and Josiah Wedgwood, in 1787. It advocated the colonization of free blacks. Sponsored by the society, three boatloads of free black settlers arrived in Sierra Leone in May of 1787. (Courtesy of The New York Public Library.)

Scotia in January 1792. Their convoy of fifteen ships arrived on the West Coast of Africa in March 1792, and Peters was among those who landed at Kru Bay. Their new home was called "Freetown."

Pragmatically, the success of the antislavery and abolitionist movements in England was due to economic and political considerations. Great Britain had recognized that eventually the slave-trade system would break down and collapse. With increased mechanization and the success of the Industrial Revolution, the British no longer needed this trade to bolster their economy. By policing the trade along the West Coast of Africa, chasing illegal traffickers and returning emigrants to new settlements, England could now turn her attention to establishing normal trade relations with Africa. So, in the late eighteenth and early nineteenth centuries, England ushered in the era of Christianity, commerce, and colonization to the African continent.

THE FOUNDING OF LIBERIA

Presidents from Jefferson to Lincoln were convinced that emancipation and colonization were inseparable issues. Jefferson himself was ambivalent on the subject of abolition. He described the Atlantic slave-trade system as an "execrable commerce," yet upon his death on July 4, 1826, he still held 250 slaves in bondage. Jefferson believed that blacks and whites could not live in peace within the borders of the United States. He hoped that Haiti would remain in the hands of the French, so that some free blacks could be colonized in the Caribbean while others might be returned to Africa. He watched with great interest the progress of the experiment begun at Sierra Leone by the British.

But Jefferson's plans were frustrated by the rise to power and the revolutionary activities of Toussaint L'Ouverture. During his first administration (1801-1804), Jefferson had appointed Tobias Lear, Washington's former secretary, as consul to Santo Domingo. Because of the tumult in Haiti, Lear was forced to return to America in 1802.

Jefferson's hopes for colonization of American blacks were seemingly embraced by the American Colonization Society, which was founded in 1817. Incorporated under the name "The American Society for Colonizing the Free People of Colour of the United States," the Society's aims appeared to be both charitable and benevolent. But further study reveals that among the American Colonization Society's membership and governing board, there was a vast division of thought and feeling on the subject of slavery and the slave trade. Among the members there were those who (1) adamantly opposed slavery and wished to offer free blacks a refuge from oppression; (2) wished to increase the value of their own slaves by ridding themselves of troublesome free blacks; and (3) wished to be relieved of any responsibility whatsoever for the rights of free blacks as members of the body politic.

The American Colonization Society (or A.C.S.) widely publicized the belief that its aims were beneficial to blacks and would unite the country. Seeming to offer something for everybody, state organizations sprang up in both North and South. But the Society made it abundantly clear that it had no intention of disturbing the system of slavery and was not an antislavery or abolitionist organization.

Captain Paul Cuffe (1758-1817) at his own expense transported thirty-eight families to Sierra Leone in West Africa, two years before the founding of the American Colonization Society in 1817. Born near New Bedford, Massachusetts, Paul renounced the family slave name and took his father's first name, Cuffe, as his surname as a free man. Through his own efforts he became a wealthy shipowner. Cuffe attempted to establish trade relations between England, the United States, and Sierra Leone. Like others, he believed that the establishment of normal commercial relations would help significantly in ending the slave trade. Cuffe also proposed the growing of cotton in these new settlements by free blacks to reduce the need for slave labor in the Caribbean and the American states. (Courtesy of The Old Dartmouth Historical Society Whaling Museum, New Bedford, Massachusetts.)

While incorporated as a private organization, the A.C.S. had very strong ties with the Congress, and it was often difficult to separate private concerns from national policies. Henry Clay, then Speaker of the House of Representatives, presided over the organizational meeting. Bushrod Washington of Mount Vernon was elected the first president. William Thornton, architect, inventor, and designer of the United States Capitol, was a member of the Society's Board of Managers. Much of official Washington had become actively involved with the Society when, in 1827, it convened its tenth annual meeting in the Capital City.

The report to the A.C.S. convention of 1827 by the Reverend R. R. Gurley, the Society's resident agent, concluded on the positive note that the colony was prevailing, and there was an increased spirit of obedience, industry, enterprise, and piety among the emigrants. Further, by this date, homes, schools, and churches had been constructed, self-government was evolving, and the settlers were productively engaged in agriculture and husbandry.

Even with the encouraging reports and the projection of success in Liberia, the black community was not of one mind on the issue of colonization. Some free blacks believed it to be an evil scheme that was designed to force their deportation from the American shores—shores which they considered to be their home. But for many of the four million slaves (most of whom were plantation slaves in the Deep South), colonization became the only hope of emancipation. With no alternative, for many deportation seemed infinitely better than perpetual bondage. The issue ultimately divided old comrades in the fight against slavery, some of whom could not accept colonization as *the* solution to their many and vexing problems without first attacking the root causes of the problems. These they considered to be the continuation of

The Reverend Daniel Coker, a free black from Baltimore, was the first elected bishop of the African Methodist Episcopal Church in Philadelphia. Coker, however, did not serve and supported the nomination of Richard Allen in his place. In 1820, Coker became a leader of the Sherbro Island settlers. An agent for the American Colonization Society, Coker kept a diary of his experiences while at Foura Bay, West Africa, in 1821. (Courtesy of The Historical Society of Pennsylvania.)

Edward Wilmot Blyden (1832-1912), a native of St. Thomas, Virgin Islands—then the Danish West Indies—was among the early proponents of Pan-Africanism. After emigrating with his brother to Liberia in 1851, Blyden became an educator and served as Liberia's minister to England from 1877 to 1881. A correspondent with the New York State Colonization Society, Blyden urged that only "the purest African" be selected for colonization in Africa. He noted the high mortality rate among those of mixed blood, whom he described as a "degenerate stock." Blyden also corresponded with Joseph Henry, Secretary of the Smithsonian Institution. A letter addressed to the Secretary, a lifetime member of the American Colonization Society, was published in the *Smithsonian Institution's Annual Report* for 1870 and entitled "On Mixed Races In Liberia." (Courtesy of the Library of Congress, Prints and Photographs Division.)

the illegal foreign trafficking in slaves by the United States and the strengthening of the domestic slave trade through the sale of slaves from the industrial North to the agrarian South. Later, this differing of opinion created a chasm in the national black leadership and finally became the catalyst for the Negro Convention Movement. Clearly making the distinction between themselves and those blacks who returned to Africa under the auspices of colonization societies, free blacks like Martin Delany and Henry Highland Garnet began calling themselves emigrationists.

Between 1828 and 1838, a new wave of emigrants embarked for the coast of West Africa. These families came under the auspices of state organizations or local branches of the American Colonization Society. The Grand Bassa settlement, located at the entrance of the St. John's River, was founded with the assistance of the

New York and Pennsylvania Colonization societies. Approximately one-hundred miles south of Monrovia, the settlement of Greenville developed at the entrance of the Sino River. Since most of the emigrants who populated this colony came from Mississippi, the colony was known as "Mississippi in Africa." A hundred miles farther south, there developed the town of Harper[18] at the Maryland Colony. This settlement on Cape Palmas was near the Cavalla River. Because of the distances between them, these settlements were at first independent.

In 1838, all of the settlements except the Maryland Colony became the "Commonwealth of Liberia." Maryland remained an independent settlement until 1857. Following a constitutional convention, Liberia issued a Declaration of Independence on July 27, 1847; she also adopted the Constitution of the Liberian Republic. With this stroke, Liberia became the first independent republic on the continent of Africa. In October of 1847, Joseph Jenkins Roberts—a mulatto from Petersburg, Virginia, and an early emigrant to Liberia—was elected the first president of the republic. The seal chosen by the new republic tells us, not only why nearly fifteen-thousand blacks eventually emigrated from America to their motherland, but why they persevered. The motto states simply: THE LOVE OF LIBERTY BROUGHT US HERE.

The seal selected for the new black Republic of Liberia in 1847 bore the motto: The Love Of Liberty Brought Us Here. (Courtesy Howard University, Moorland-Spingarn Research Center.)

---

[18]The town of Harper was named for Robert Goodloe Harper, who suggested the name *Liberia* for the new country of liberated Africans. It was also Harper who suggested that the capital city, Monrovia, be named for President James Monroe.

PICTORIAL ESSAY

THE QUEST

Out of Africa moves from West Africa to the European colonies in the Caribbean and North America and back to Africa again. The story it tells—complex, tragic, sometimes heroic—can be told in terms of written history. It can also be told in terms of the physical evidence of the people and places involved. Artifacts, documents, maps, portraits, photographs, all speak eloquently of the triumph and destruction of West African civilization and the experience and achievement of the Africans who were brought to the Americas.

The following pictorial essay presents their story. It is divided into twelve sections. Together, they trace a significant portion of the shared histories of Africa and America. If we are to understand the history and culture of either, then we must understand the history and culture of both, for they are permanently linked. These pictures provide the reader with yet another approach to this vital subject.

An Ashanti chief dressed in Kente cloth with gold jewelry. Photographs courtesy of the Museum of African Art, Eliot Elisofon Archives.

Homes of the Dogon people on a hillside in present-day Mali.

Yoruba dancers wearing *Gelede* masks perform in a ceremony in Nigeria.

Egungun mask of the Yoruba people of Nigeria. Included on this headdress is a replica of the talking drum, which is used to relay messages from one drummer to another. Drummers can communicate over distances of a hundred miles or more.

Prince Henry the Navigator (1394-1450) of Portugal.

A European map of 1375, showing West Africa. In the lower right is Mansa Musa, holding a scepter and a piece of gold. The map describes Mansa Musa as "the richest and most noble king in all the land." (Photographs courtesy of the Bibliothèque Nationale, Paris, France.)

A Nupe village in Nigeria.

Tuaregs crossing the desert in Nigeria. (Photographs courtesy of the Museum of African Art, Eliot Elisofon Archives.)

Upper left, "Am I Not a Man and a Brother?" This antislavery medallion was created by the English potter Josiah Wedgwood in 1778 and sent to Benjamin Franklin. (Photograph courtesy of Dr. Lloyd E. Hawes)

Above, copper slave identification tags used in public slave auctions held at Charleston, South Carolina, between 1831 and 1849. (Courtesy The Chicago Public Library, Special Collections Division, Grand Army Hall and Memorial Association Collection.)

Peter Williams (1748-1824), one of the founders of the African Methodist Episcopal Zion Church. Born a slave, Williams was sold in 1778 to the trustees of the John Street Methodist Episcopal Church in New York, where he worked as a sexton. He purchased his own freedom in 1785. A supporter of Paul Cuffe, Williams organized the African Institute in New York. (Courtesy John Street United Methodist Church.)

Very little is known about Thomas Howland, a Providence, Rhode Island, merchant and an emigrant to Liberia. The first black ever elected to public office by popular vote in the city of Providence, Howland first appears in the listings of the Providence city directory in 1832. In spite of his apparent affluence and his success as the popular warden of the third ward in Providence, Howland left Rhode Island and relocated his family in Africa in 1857. (Courtesy The Rhode Island Historical Society.)

Through words and pictures, we continue our quest to recover and reexamine black history. The story moves from the glories of West Africa—its beauty, history, and culture—to the coming of the European, through the villainy of slavery, and the determined effort of those who opposed it. Thence, there is a return to Africa with those who tried to build new lives for themselves in the land of their ancestors.

ANCIENT KINGDOMS

Ancient West Africa produced several great cultures. For centuries these cultures would remain largely unknown to the Western world.

The following maps show Europeans' changing conceptions of Africa. The first map dates from 1450. The unrecognizable continent of Africa is on the bottom half of the map. On the lower left, five rivers flow into a great lake near Timbuktu. The second map dates from 1490 and displays a much more sophisticated knowledge of Africa's west coast as far as the Cape of Good Hope. As this map shows, the east coast of Africa was still unexplored. Map number three was drawn in 1561 and gives a fairly complete picture of the shape of the continent. The interior of Africa is fanciful, though: in the middle of the continent sits a "Monoculi," a one-eyed man, said to inhabit the region near the mythical Mountains of the Moon. At the bottom of the map is a sixteenth-century sailing vessel of the type being used to explore the African continent. The last map dates from 1671. It is detailed and realistic in its treatment of the coastal areas, though much of the interior shown here is incorrect. Of special interest is the cartouche on the lower left, which bears witness to the rich trade going on between Europe and Africa at this time.

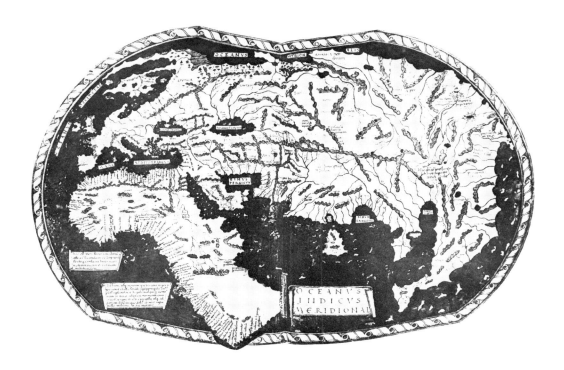

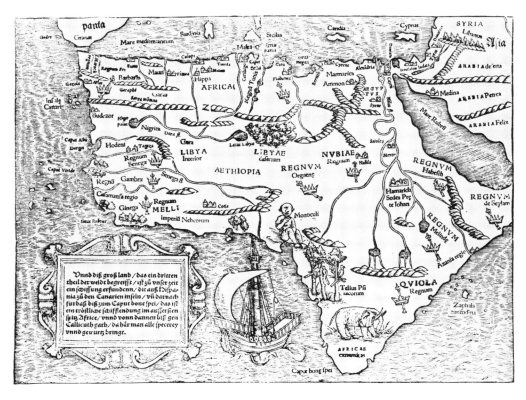

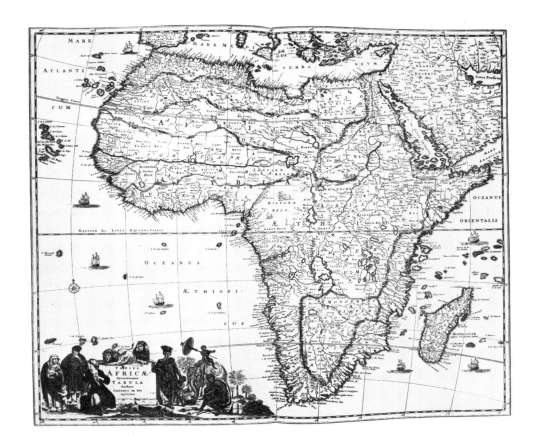

Caravans linked West Africa with other parts of the continent and, ultimately, with Europe. (Courtesy of the Museum of African Art, Eliot Elisofon Archives.)

A drawing of Timbuktu believed to have been made by one of the first Europeans to visit it. The city's design was functional—because of the direction of the prevalent winds, its streets were all laid out in one direction. (From *African Glory* by J. C. DeGraft-Johnson.)

Two Hausa horsemen and a musician. (Courtesy of the Museum of African Art, Eliot Elisofon Archives.)

ART OF WEST AFRICA

Social identity is a vital force in African life. It is preserved by closely held traditions within many groups and subgroups, each with its own language and culture. These traditions find expression in the art of Africa.

Goldweights of the Ashanti people of Ghana. Used to measure gold dust, these weights are individually cast in bronze. A language of pictures or hieroglyphics, the miniature pieces often represent objects of daily use. Others embody proverbs or philosophical concepts reflecting ancient traditions. Some are inscribed with symbols of plant life, animals, and birds. Much of Ashanti history and culture can be learned by interpreting the goldweights. (Courtesy of the Museum of African Art.)

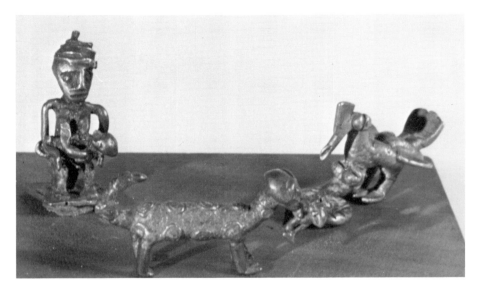

Decorative spoon of the Mende people of Sierra Leone. These elaborate pieces are objects of beauty as well as utility. (Courtesy of the Museum of African Art.)

Decorative spoon from the Bambara people of Mali. (Courtesy of the Museum of African Art.)

These brass figures from the Ivory Coast are fine examples of African craftsmanship. The two seated figures are only 1½ inches high; the standing figure is 1⅝ inches high. (Courtesy of the Metropolitan Museum of Art, The Michael C. Rockefeller Collection of Primitive Art on loan from Nelson A. Rockefeller.)

86

Bronze sculpture, *Execution Group,* from Benin. The Nigerian kingdom of Benin, located in midwestern Nigeria, flourished from the fifteenth through the nineteenth century, and was renowned for the excellence of its bronze casting. (Courtesy of the Hirshhorn Museum and Sculpture Garden, Smithsonian Institution.)

Dancer wearing a *Chi Wara* headdress. Pairs of male dancers wear male and female head-dresses at planting and harvest ceremonies. (Courtesy of the Museum of African Art, Eliot Elisofon Archives.)

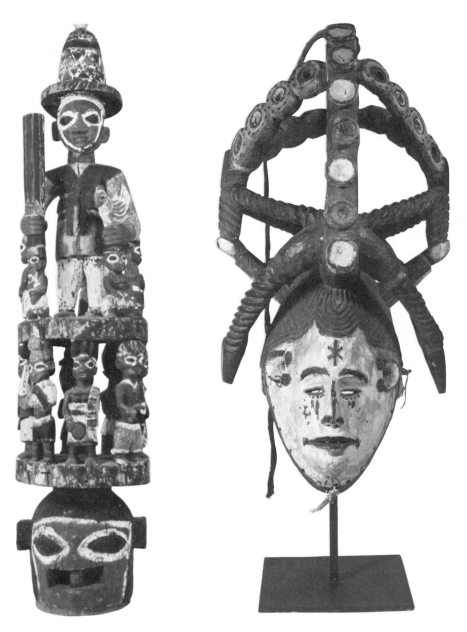

Epa mask of the Yoruba people of Nigeria. These large masks are carved in a variety of forms for the rituals of the *Epa* Society. At the end of one ceremony, a masked dancer leaps onto a mound. If he remains upright with the heavy weight on his head, good fortune will come to the community. If he falls, rituals must be performed to appease the spirits who have been offended. (Courtesy of the Museum of African Art.)

Mmwo Society mask of the Ibo people of Nigeria. The *Mmwo* (soul) is the most important men's society among the Ibo. Young men wear the masks at the funeral rites that make their fathers members of *Mmwo* in the spirit world. After the ceremony, the sons become members of the Society. (Courtesy of the Museum of African Art.)

A *Gelede* Society mask of the Yoruba people of Nigeria. Worn by pairs of dancers in religious ceremonies, each mask has a different design. One important ceremony, the annual festival honoring *Odudua*, the earth goddess, appeases witches and insures the fertility of women. (Courtesy of the Museum of African Art.)

Female figure carved by the Senufo people of the Ivory Coast. This seated figure with enlarged breasts and swollen belly symbolizes fertility, an important concept throughout Africa. (Courtesy of the Museum of African Art.)

Shango staff carved by the Yoruba people of Nigeria. These staffs are used in ceremonies to invoke the spirit of *Shango,* the Yoruba god of thunder. The female form depicts the god's wife *Oya* wearing a headdress in the form of a double axe. (Courtesy of the Museum of African Art.)

Equestrian figure carved by the Senufo people of the Ivory Coast. Ancestors were often depicted riding horses, which were rare in parts of West Africa and thus became symbols of power and authority. (Courtesy of the Museum of African Art.)

Helmet mask ("Firespitter") of the Senufo people of the Ivory Coast. These masks represent the spirits of many different animals and are worn in the performance of agricultural, educational, and funeral rites. (Courtesy of the Museum of African Art.)

90

THE SLAVE TRADE

The brutal slave trade was a carefully managed enterprise, as these pictures and documents show.

The plan of the lower deck of the slave ship *Brookes* allowed for stowage of 292 slaves. Of this number 130 were stowed under the shelves as shown in Fig. 5.

Fig. 3 shows how additional slaves were stowed around the wings or sides of the lower deck by means of platforms or shelves—in the manner of galleries in a church. The space for the slaves stowed on the shelves has a height of only 2 feet 7 inches between the beams, less under the beams.

After the Regulation Act of 1788, the *Brookes* was allowed to carry 454 slaves. She could stow this number by following the rule adopted in this illustration, namely of allowing a space of 6 feet by 1 foot 4 inches to each man, 5 feet 10 inches by 1 foot 4 inches to each woman, and 5 feet by 1 foot 2 inches to each boy; but so much space as this was seldom allowed even after the Regulation Act. It was proved by the confession of a slave merchant that before the Regulations Act, the *Brookes* had at one time carried as many as 609 slaves. This was done by taking some out of irons and stowing one within the distended legs of the other. (Courtesy of the National Park Service, American Museum of Immigration, Statue of Liberty.)

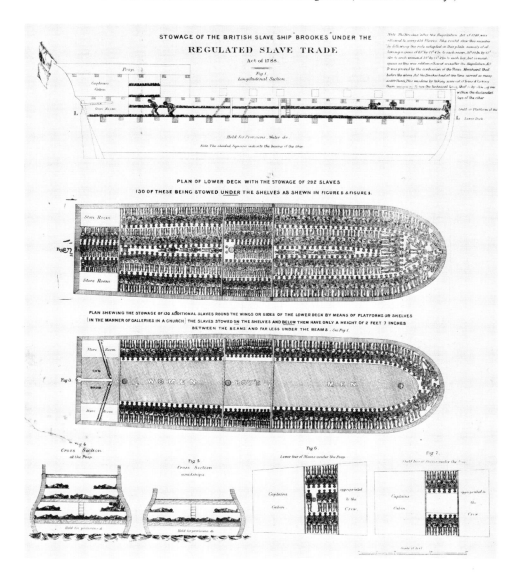

It is agreed between the Master, Seamen, and Mariners of the *Sloop Adventure, whereof Samuel Tuell is* ——— Master, now bound from *Barbadoes to Charles Town in South Carolina and from thence to Newport in Rhode Island*

That in Confideration of the monthly or other Wages againſt each refpective Seaman and Mariner's Name hereunder ſet, they do and will perform the abovementioned Voyage; and the ſaid Maſter doth hereby agree with, and hire the ſaid Seamen and Mariners for the ſaid Voyage, at ſuch monthly Wages, to be paid purſuant to the Laws of *Great-Britain*: And they the ſaid Seamen and Mariners do hereby promiſe and oblige themſelves to do their Duty, and obey the lawful Commands of their Officers on board the ſaid *Sloop* ——— or the Boats thereto belonging, as becomes good and faithful Seamen and Mariners; and that at all the Places where the ſaid *Sloop* ——— ſhall put in, or anchor at, during the ſaid Voyage; and to do their beſt Endeavours for the Preſervation of the ſaid *Sloop* ——— and Cargo, and do not neglect or refuſe doing their Duty by Day or Night, nor go out of the ſaid *Sloop* ——— on board any other Veſſel, or on Shore under any Pretence whatſoever, without Leave firſt obtained of the Captain or Commanding Officer on board: That in Default thereof, they will not only be liable to the Penalties mentioned in an Act of Parliament made in the ſecond Year of the Reign of King GEORGE the Second, &c. intitled, *An Act for the better Regulation and Government of Seamen in the Merchants Service*, but will further, in Caſe they ſhould on any Account whatſoever leave or deſert the ſaid *Sloop* ——— without the Maſter's Conſent, till the aboveſaid Voyage be ended, and the ſaid *Sloop* be diſcharged of her Loading, be liable to forfeit and loſe what Wages may at ſuch Time of their Deſertion be due to them, together with every their Goods, Chattels, &c. on board, renouncing by theſe Preſents all Title, Right, Demand, and Pretenſion thereunto for ever, for them, their Heirs, Executors, and Adminiſtrators. And it is further agreed by both Parties, that eight and forty Hours Abſence, without Leave, ſhall be deemed a total Deſertion, and render ſuch Seamen and Mariners liable to the Penalties abovementioned. That each and every lawful Command which the ſaid Maſter ſhall think neceſſary hereafter to iſſue, for the effectual Government of the ſaid Veſſel, ſuppreſſing Immorality and Vice of all Kinds, be ſtrictly complied with under Penalty of the Perſon or Perſons diſobeying, forfeiting his or their whole Wages, or Hire, together with every Thing belonging to him or them on board the ſaid Veſſel. And it is further agreed on, that no Officer nor Seaman belonging to the ſaid *Sloop* ——— ſhall demand or be intitled to his Wages, or any Part thereof, until the Arrival of the ſaid *Sloop* ——— at the abovementioned Port of Diſcharge in *Newport aforesaid* ——— That each Seaman and Mariner who ſhall well and truly perform the abovementioned Voyage (provided always, that there be no Plunderage, Embezzlement, or other unlawful Acts committed on ſaid Veſſel's Cargo or Stores) be intitled to the Wages or Hire that may be due to him, purſuant to this Agreement. That for the due Performance of each and every of the abovementioned Articles, and as an Agreement and Acknowledgment of their being voluntarily, and without Compulſion, or any clandeſtine Means being uſed, agreed to, and ſigned by us, we have, in Teſtimony thereof, each and every of us, hereunder ſigned our Hands, the Month and Day againſt each Name affixed, and in the Year of our Lord, 1773 ———

Times of Entry.	MEN's NAMES.	Quality.	Witneſſes to each Man's ſigning.	Advance Wages before ſailing.	Wages per Month.	Whole Wages. £. | s. | d
March — 1	Tho. Danforth	Seaman	Robert Clark	2 : 3 : 9	2 : 3 : 9	
march — 12	Samuel Fosset	do.	Robt Champlin	1 : 11 : 3	1 : 11 : 3	
march — 13	Charles Jones	ditto	Robt Champlin Run			
march — 22	Jno Reed	ditto	Robt Champlin	2 : 3 : 9	2 : 3 : 9	

A ship's manifest for the slave ship *Adventure,* listing the crew, wages, and length of service. The *Adventure* sailed from Barbados to Charleston, South Carolina, and then to Newport, Rhode Island, in 1772 and 1773. (Courtesy of the Columbia University Libraries, George Arthur Plimpton Manuscript Collection.)

An Account of the Number of Negroes delivered in to the Islands of Barbadoes, Jamaica, and Antego, from the Year 1698 to 1708. since the Trade was Opened, taken from the Accounts sent from the respective Governours of those Islands to the Lords Commissioners of Trade, whereby it appears the African Trade is encreas'd to four times more since its being laid Open, than it was under an Exclusive Company.

Between what Years deliver'd.	N°. of Negroes delivered into Barbados.	Number delivered into Jamaica.	Number delivered into Antego.
Between the 8 April, 1698 To April 1699 }	3436		
To April 1700	3080		
To 5 ditto 1701	4311		
To 10 ditto 1702	9213		
To 31 Mar. 1703	4561		
To 5 April 1704	1876		
To 2d. ditto 1705	3319		
To 5 ditto 1706	1875		
To 12 May 1707	2720		
To 29 April 1708	1018		
Between 29 Sept. - - 1698 and 29 Decemb. 1698 }		1273	
Between 7 April - - 1699 and 28 March 1700 }		5766	
From 28 Mar. to 3 Apr. 1701		6068	
3 Apr. 1701. to 20 dit. 1702		8505	
20 dit. 1702 to 12 dit. 1703		2238	
12 dit. 1703 to 18 dit. 1704		2711	
18 dit. 1704 to 24 dit. 1705		3421	
24 dit. 1705 to 27 dit. 1706		5462	
27 dit. 1706 to 22 dit. 1707		2122	
22 dit. 1707 to 26 dit. 1708		6623	
To June 1708		187	
1698			18
June 1699			212
Between June - - 1700 and 24 April 1701 }			364
Between 24 April - 1701 and 30 March 1702 }			2395
To April 1703			1670
To Nov. 1704			1551
To 1705			269
To 1706			530
To 1707			114
	35409	44376	7123

Besides which there are 7 Separate Ships named in the foregoing List for *Antego*, but not the Number of Negroes, so we may well compute them at 1200 more, which arriv'd between 1699 and 1700.

A

An

''An Account of the Number of Negroes delivered in to the Islands of Barbadoes, Jamaica, and Antego, from the Year 1698 to 1708. . . . Sent from the respective Governours of those Islands to the Lord Commissioners of Trade . . . it appears the African Trade is encreas'd to four times more since its being laid Open, than it was under Exclusive Company.'' (Courtesy of The Historical Society of Pennsylvania.)

An Account of the Number of Negroes delivered by the Royal African Company, *between* 1698. *and* 1707. *given in to the* Lords Commissioners of Trade *by the said Company.*

Years.	Number of Negroes imported by the Company.
1698	941
1699	1500
1700	2045
1701	1511
1702	2014
1703	1138
1704	2745
1705	2921
1706	1144
1707	1801
	17760

From the foregoing Account, given in by the Company, 'tis plain how many Negroes they imported Annually. So it must naturally follow, that what more than these were delivered into the Plantations, in that time, must be on Account of the Separate Traders.

Also from the Account of Negroes delivered in to *Barbadoes, Jamaica,* and *Antego,* it appears, that the Numbers imported into those three Islands, (allowing 1200 for the said 7 Ships, whose Numbers are not included by the Governour of *Antego* in his Account) amount to 88108. And even allowing the whole Number which the *African* Company sent out, being 17760, were all deliver'd at those three Islands only, yet then it appears, the Separate Traders have delivered 70 odd Thousand to the Company's 17760, in about the same time, besides what were delivered into *Virginia, Maryland,* and all the other Colonies, which must amount to at least thirty or forty Thousand more.

It appears also from the said Account, that there were imported into those 3 Colonies only 42000 and odd Negroes in the Years 1700, 1701, and 1702, whereof not above 4000 by the *African* Company, which being compared with the Company's Imports of Negroes into all the Plantations, when Exclusive, between 1680 and 1688, amounting but to 46396, or 5150 Negroes *per An.* as is to be seen by their own Account, given in to the Lords Commissioners of Trade. It is very plain, there were near as many Negroes deliver'd into those 3 Plantations in 3 Years, since the Trade was open'd, as were deliver'd in 9 Years by the Company into all the Plantations, when Exclusive to all others.

It farther appears from the said Account, that there were more Negroes deliver'd into those 3 Plantations in one Year by Separate Traders, between *April* 1701, and *April* 1702. being 18602, than the Company deliver'd in the nine Years and half since the Act, being 17760, because the Total of Negroes, imported both by the Company and Separate Traders in that Year, amounted to 20113, out of which, deducting even the full Number deliver'd by them into all the Plantations that same Year, being 1511, the Remainder is above 18602.

Again, It must be observed, that the Import of Negroes in that Year for those 3 Colonies only, are within 2000 and odd of as many as the Company deliver'd in 4 Years, when Exclusive (even in time of Peace) into all the Plantations.

An account of the number of Negroes delivered by the Royal African Company between 1698 and 1708. (Courtesy of The Historical Society of Pennsylvania.)

British Museum - Add. MSS. N.º 15.485 –

Account of the number of vessels with their tonnage that have entered inwards & cleared outwards in the sev.ª provinces of N. America × × × between 5 Jan.y 1768 & 5 Jan.y 1769.

In		Out	In		Out
34	Topsails	62	22	Topsails	10
3	Sloops & c	2	289	Sloops & c	237
4953	Tonnage	7890	10.211	Tonnage	7.040
for Great Britain		××	for Cont.l of Am., Bahamas & c		
9	Topsails	14	33	Topsails	41
2	Sloops & c	4	80	Sloops & c	115
1065	Tonnage	1106	5300	Tonnage	6.869
for So. p.ts of Europe & africa			for Brit.h & Forgn. W. Indies		

N.º Carolina

Exported to G. Britain

133 Bush. Flax Seed
7.800 „ Corn
621 „ „ Rice
9.5.1.14 Hemp
646 tt Indigo
4 Tons Lignum Vitae
5.º 126 Oil
3.808 B.l.s Pitch
57.658 „ Naval Stores (? Rosin)
9.863 „ „ „ (? Tarpt)
4.7.2 Bread & Flour
2 cwt. Bacon
11.700 Reeds
1488 tt 55 Cases 41 Hhds & 2469 Raw Deer
352 Hhds. Tobacco

1500 tt Wax
219 galls Wine
6 Bales & 214 tt Whale Skins
205.405. ft Lumber
1000 ft Boards & Oak Plank 39 inches
22 Tons Spars
200 Hoops
435.805 Staves
3.000 Shingles
3.000 Oars & Rafters
482 Tons Pine
224 Hawk Spikes
180 ft & 19 Logs Cedar

This Book is full of & detailed tabular statements of G.t Imports &c Browne

From the records of the British Museum, an account of the number of vessels, with their tonnage, that entered the ports of the Carolinas between January 5, 1768, and January 5, 1769. The vessels were carrying cargo received in exchange for slaves. (Courtesy, DeRosset Family Papers, Southern Historical Collection, University of North Carolina Library, Chapel Hill.)

Rebellious slaves being thrown overboard during the Middle Passage. (Courtesy of the Library of Congress, Prints and Photographs Division.)

Resistance to slavery began even before the arrival of slaves in the Caribbean, or in America. Neck and wrist irons like these were used during the Middle Passage to subdue any slave who might become violent. (Courtesy of the National Park Service, American Museum of Immigration, Statue of Liberty National Monument.)

Captured and yoked Africans on a forced march. (Courtesy of Howard University, Moorland-Spingarn Research Center.)

An African slave coffle on its way to the coast. (Courtesy of the National Museum of History and Technology, Smithsonian Institution.)

First named São Jorge Castle and later called Elmina, this fort was built during the Portuguese period, with work begun in the late fifteenth century. Most of the stone used in the construction came from the site and artisans were brought from Portugal. According to an African legend, while the men were at work they were attacked by the people of Elmina, who were angered that a sacred place had been disturbed. A shrine was then built in one of the vaults of the castle to appease the spirit of the rock. (Courtesy of the Library of Congress, Prints and Photographs Division.)

A courtyard in Elmina Castle. Columbus may have had a hand in the construction of this European fort, the first to be built in Africa. (Courtesy of Reginald Jackson and Ted Pontiflet. Copyright 1977.)

Cape Coast Castle as seen from the shore. (Courtesy of Reginald Jackson and Ted Pontiflet. Copyright 1977.)

View of Cape Coast Castle, one of the slave forts built between the mid-seventeenth century and the end of the eighteenth. These pictures give some idea of the massive scale of the structures that held captured Africans who would be transported to the colonies of the New World. (Courtesy of Reginald Jackson and Ted Pontiflet. Copyright 1977.)

A hilltop site near Kormantine was allocated to the English for the purpose of building a small fortified lodge, which was destroyed by fire in 1640. The Dutch later occupied the site and built Fort Amsterdam. This fort is believed to be the first of the forts built specifically to serve as a slave-prison on the west coast of Africa. Even after the English lost possession of the site to the Dutch, British West Indian planters continued to refer to slaves from the Gold Coast as ''Cormantins.'' (Courtesy of Reginald Jackson and Ted Pontiflet. Copyright 1977.)

Begun by the English in 1660, Fort Carolusburg was completed in 1665. By 1690 it was familiarly known as Cape Coast Castle. Modified and enlarged about 1780, the north side of the wall was extended to what is still known today as ''Greenhill's Point.'' In order to protect the only place where canoes could safely land, a long platform was mounted with many guns. Slaves were kept underground to guard against insurrections. (Courtesy of Reginald Jackson and Ted Pontiflet. Copyright 1977.)

Ruins of the slave fort at St. James Island, the first slave fort built by the French, at the mouth of the Gambia and Senegal rivers. (Courtesy of Fletcher A. Smith.)

Since 1638 the French had made several unsuccessful attempts to establish themselves on the West Coast of Africa, but had been unable to compete with the Dutch and English, who arrived before them. A French trade-post of six houses was burned by the Dutch only a month after completion.

During the eighteenth century few new forts were built; however, in October 1755 the plan for the construction of a fort by the French on the Gambia had been completed. Events in eighteenth-century France and their Caribbean colony Haiti resulted in a change in the attitudes of Frenchmen toward the institution of slavery and the trade.

SLAVE LIFE IN THE CARIBBEAN

These scenes illustrate some of the conditions of slave life in Jamaica.

A Negro market in Jamaica. (Courtesy of the West India Reference Library, Institute of Jamaica.)

Slaves on a treadmill in Jamaica. (Courtesy of the Library of Congress, Prints and Photographs Division.)

Slaves cutting cane on a sugar plantation in Jamaica. (Courtesy of the West India Reference Library, Institute of Jamaica.)

Slaves at work in a boiling house on a sugar plantation in Jamaica. (Courtesy of the West India Reference Library, Institute of Jamaica.)

Molasses in barrels being loaded on ships leaving Jamaica. (Courtesy of the West India Reference Library, Institute of Jamaica.)

SLAVERY IN THE UNITED STATES

The following pictures and documents are evidence of the oppressive economic system of slavery that developed in the United States. As early as the seventeenth century, African slaves imported into the American colonies began to resist the yoke. In Northern cities as well as on Southern plantations, resistance was spearheaded by slaves who were sometimes joined by white indentured servants. In 1712, in New York, rebel slaves killed nine whites in a street confrontation. A rumor that slaves and indentured servants planned to revolt in New York in 1741 resulted in atrocities being committed against blacks and whites.

The lives of slaves and free blacks were regulated by a complex web of laws. State and national laws—the ''black codes''—came into play whenever blacks were bòrn or died, bought or sold, or when they wished to marry or gather together. Throughout the colonies slave codes became more stringent, yet the master's unquestionable right to control his slaves only served to intensify their restlessness.

New York slave market about 1730. (Courtesy of the New York Public Library.)

Sworn testimony concerning the delivery of a slave in Boston, April 6, 1697. (Courtesy of the Columbia University Libraries, George Arthur Plimpton Manuscript Collection.)

This advertisement, dated October 4, 1760, asks for the return of a slave. Calling himself Silas Williams, the fugitive ran away from his master in Middletown, Connecticut, in 1754. (Courtesy of the State Historical Society of Wisconsin.)

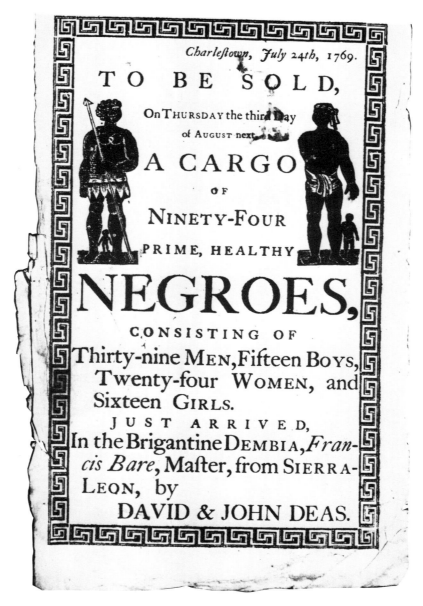

Charlestown, July 24th, 1769.

TO BE SOLD,

On THURSDAY the third Day
of AUGUST next,

A CARGO
OF
NINETY-FOUR
PRIME, HEALTHY

NEGROES,

CONSISTING OF
Thirty-nine MEN, Fifteen BOYS,
Twenty-four WOMEN, and
Sixteen GIRLS.
JUST ARRIVED,
In the Brigantine DEMBIA, *Francis Bare*, Master, from SIERRA-
LEON, by
DAVID & JOHN DEAS.

The years between 1748 and 1775 were the time of the greatest importation of slaves from Africa to Charles Town (now Charleston), South Carolina. A sign of prosperity among the planters, this new wealth gave rise to a successful merchant class that included the brothers David and John Deas. Emigrants from Scotland in 1738 and 1749 respectively, David and John were co-partners in the firm of Lennox & Deas, importers of a variety of goods from Europe and India. By April of 1749, their inventory included rum and some hogsheads (barrels) of "good muscavado sugar" from Jamaica.

In 1763 it was announced that the Deas partnership was dissolving; yet this broadside appeared on July 24, 1769. John Deas also inherited slaves through his marriage to Elizabeth Allen in 1759. In his will dated January 5, 1782, Deas provided for the perpetual bondage of his slaves. (Courtesy of the Columbia University Libraries, George Arthur Plimpton Collection.)

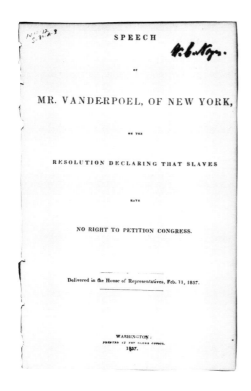

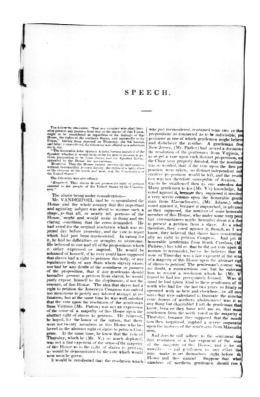

Speech of Mr. Vanderpoel, of New York, on the Resolution Declaring That Slaves Have No Right To Petition Congress which was delivered in the House of Representatives on February 11, 1837. In response to the query of John Quincy Adams as to whether it would be in order for him to present "a petition purporting to be *from slaves*," the Speaker appealed to the House for instructions. The following resolutions were presented:

"*Resolved,* That the House cannot receive said petition without disregarding its own dignity, the rights of a large class of the citizens of the south and west, and the Constitution of the United States.

"*Resolved,* That slaves do not possess the right of petition secured to the people of the United States by the Constitution." (Courtesy Cornell University Libraries, Department of Manuscripts and University Archives.)

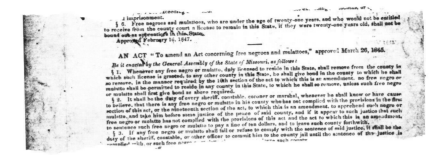

This Missouri act of 1847 is typical of the laws that denied slaves all civil rights and limited the movement of free blacks. (Courtesy of the Missouri Historical Society.)

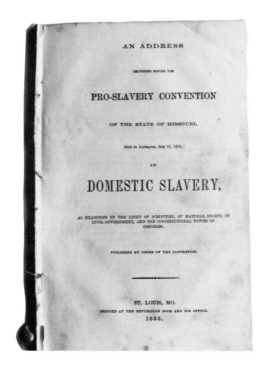

This publication was produced by the Pro-Slavery Convention of Missouri in 1855. Just as slavery had its opponents, it also had its defenders and apologists. (Courtesy of the Tennessee Disciples of Christ Historical Society Library.)

110

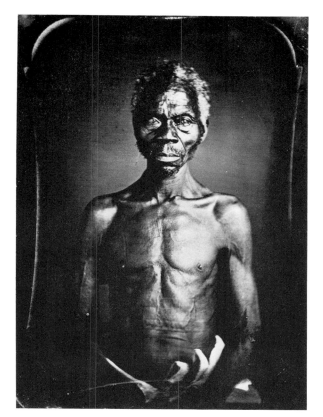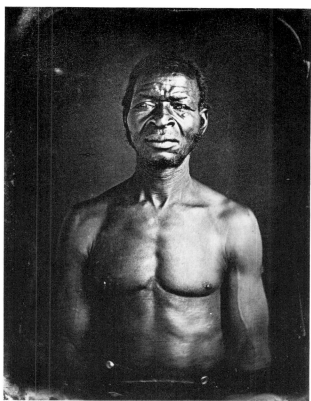

Daguerreotypes of African slaves commissioned in 1850 by Louis Agassiz, known as the father of American natural history. These daguerreotypes by J. T. Zealy were made on the plantation of B. F. Taylor of Columbia, South Carolina, ''to demonstrate the supposed inferiority of their subjects.'' (Courtesy of the Peabody Museum, Harvard University. Photograph by Hillel Burger. Copyright © President & Fellows of Harvard College, 1978.)

Preparing the cotton for the gin near Beaufort, South Carolina. (Courtesy of the National Museum of History and Technology, Smithsonian Institution.)

Slave quarters on an old South Carolina plantation. (Courtesy of The New-York Historical Society.)

Thomas Jefferson kept detailed records of the slaves at Monticello and his other outlying farms. The following excerpts from his farm book show the meticulous care with which he noted the births and deaths, locations, and the distribution of goods to them. (Permission to publish courtesy of the Massachusetts Historical Society. Photocopy of prints, courtesy of the University of Virginia Library.)

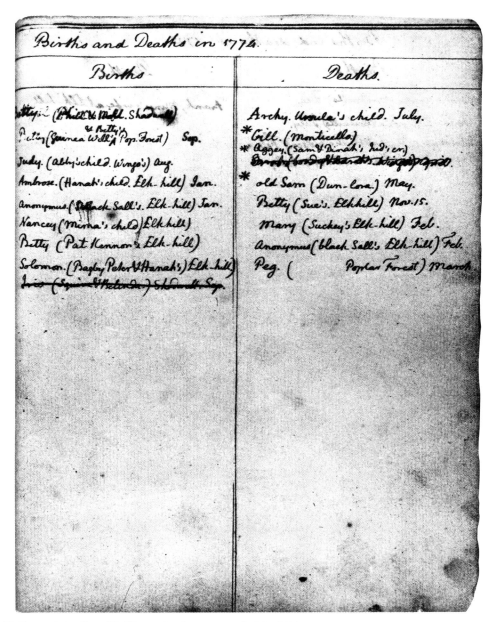

Births and deaths of Jefferson's slaves recorded in 1774.

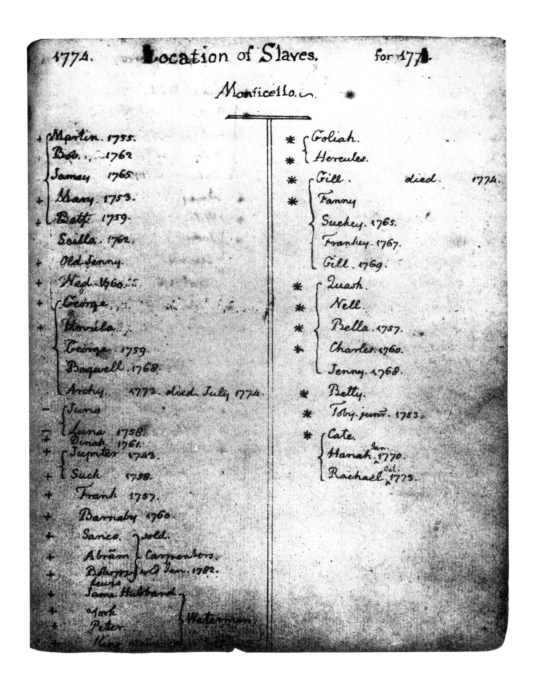

Location of slaves at Jefferson's land holdings at Monticello, Dun-lore, and Elk-Hill for the year 1774.

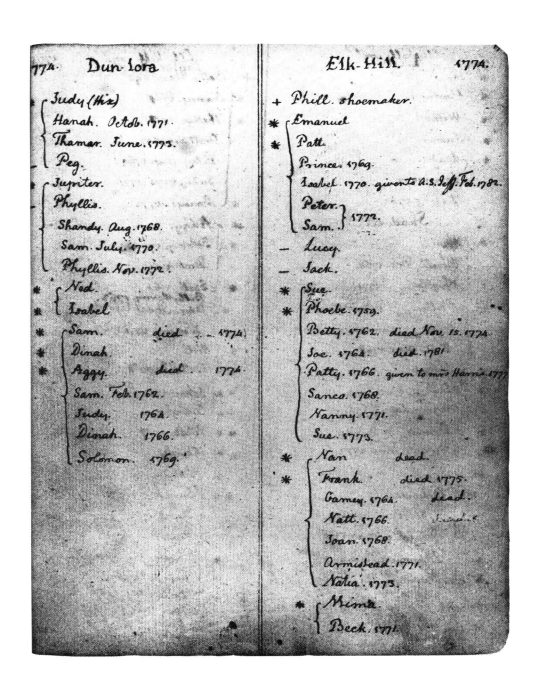

Dun-Lora 1774	Elk-Hill 1774
Judy (His)	+ Phill. shoemaker.
Hanah. Octob. 1771.	* Emanuel
Thamar. June. 1773.	* Patt.
Peg.	Prince. 1769.
Jupiter.	Isabel. 1770. given to A.S. Jeff. Feb. 1782.
Phyllis.	Peter. } 1772.
Shandy. Aug. 1768.	Sam. }
Sam. July. 1770.	— Lucy.
Phyllis. Nov. 1772.	— Jack.
* Ned.	* Sue.
* Isabel	* Phoebe. 1759.
* Sam. died 1774.	Betty. 1762. died Nov. 15. 1774.
* Dinah.	Joe. 1764. died. 1781.
* Aggy. died 1774.	Patty. 1766. given to mrs Harris 1777
Sam. Feb. 1762.	Sanco. 1768.
Judy. 1764.	Nanny. 1771.
Dinah. 1766.	Sue. 1773.
Solomon. 1769.	* Nan dead.
	* Frank. died 1775.
	Garney. 1764. dead.
	Natt. 1766.
	Joan. 1768.
	Armistead. 1771.
	Nalia. 1773.
	* Mima.
	Beck. 1771.

Blankets, beds, and other items given to Jefferson's slaves in 1776.

"Roll of the negroes taken in 1783," listing Jefferson's slaves.

Bread distributed per week among overseers and the slaves belonging to Jefferson in 1796.

An oath, dated November 1, 1778, attesting that the removal of a slave from one state to another is not for the purpose of circumventing the law, which forbade the further importation of slaves from Africa or the West Indies. (Courtesy of the State Historical Society of Wisconsin.)

Permission given by John Taylor in 1802 for his slave to marry. (Courtesy of Howard University, Moorland-Spingarn Research Center.)

In "consideration of . . . natural love and affection," Elizabeth Bennett gave slaves Jacob, Cora, and Ben to her son Bryant Bennett on May 24, 1819. (Courtesy of Howard University, Moorland-Spingarn Research Center.)

I wish to make this little book a Register of the Negroes owned by me in Buckingham; to insert their names and ages, and to note births and deaths among them. The master should know not only the names, but study the characters and ascertain the age of his slaves. It is important to know their age, because slaves over 10, and also between 12 and 16 are subjects of taxation; because this knowledge is useful and necessary in the division and distribution of property; and desirable whenever circum= =stances require that the owner should sell any of his slaves.

My sons will perhaps be glad to have this information, and that alone is a sufficient reason for my undertaking to embody and transmit it for future reference.

R. T. Hubard
Oct. 1841.

Introductory statement in R. T. Hubard's slave journal of 1841 in which he planned to record the names, ages, births, and deaths of his slaves. "It is important to know their ages, because slaves over 10 . . . are subjects of taxation; because this knowledge is . . . necessary in the . . . distribution of property. . . ." (Courtesy of the R. T. Hubard Register, University of Virginia Library.)

Tax bill of 1848 for slaves and horses owned by John K. Shore, a black man in Petersburg, Virginia. Some blacks did purchase other family members in order to obtain their freedom; however, unless free papers were obtained through the courts, technically the family member retained the status of a slave. (Courtesy of Mrs. Myra Colson Callis.)

As an economic institution, chattel slavery required the keeping of records for tax purposes. Note the ages, occupations, and values of slaves as listed in this inventory of Negroes and stock, dated December 31, 1853. (Courtesy of the George E. Grymes Manager's Journal, University of Virginia Library.)

North-Carolina Mutual Life Insurance Company.

This Policy of Insurance Witnesseth:

That THE NORTH-CAROLINA MUTUAL LIFE INSURANCE COMPANY in consideration of the sum of _____ Dollars, to them in hand paid by _____ of _____ and of the annual payment of _____ Dollars, DO INSURE the Life of _____ of _____ in the County of _____ State of _____ in the amount of _____ Dollars, for the term of _____ years, to-wit: From the _____ day of _____ one thousand eight hundred and fifty _____ at noon, to the _____ day of _____ one thousand eight hundred and _____ at noon.

And the said Company do hereby promise and agree, to and with the said Insured, _____ executors, and administrators, and assigns, well and truly to pay, or cause to be paid, the said sum insured, to the Insured, _____ executors, administrators, or assigns, within ninety days after due notice and proof of the death of the said _____.

Provided always, and it is hereby declared to be the true intent and meaning of this Policy, and the same is accepted by the Insured upon these express conditions, that in case the _____ shall, without the consent of this Company, previously obtained and endorsed upon this Policy, pass beyond the limits of the State of North Carolina, or in case the Insured shall have already any other insurance on the slave hereby insured, and not notified to this Company, and mentioned in, or endorsed upon this Policy, or shall hereafter effect any other insurance upon the said slave, without the consent of this Company, first obtained and endorsed upon this Policy; or in case the said slave shall die for want of proper medical or personal attendance, or by means of any invasion, insurrection, riot, or civil commotion, or of any military or usurped power, or by the hands of Justice; or shall die in open resistance to any authority or officer, legally constituted and appointed, or in resistance to the authority of any person or persons lawfully having the control and management of said slave; or should said slave die whilst runaway from the service of the person or persons having the control and management of him or her, then this Policy shall be void, null, and of no effect.

And it is understood and agreed to be the true intent and meaning of this Policy, that if the declaration made by the said _____ and bearing date the 11th _____ 185_, and upon the faith of which this agreement is made, shall be found in any respect untrue, then, in such case, this Policy shall be null and void.

The interest of the Insured in this Policy is not assignable, unless by consent of the Company, manifested in writing.

In Witness Whereof, The said North-Carolina Mutual Life Insurance Company have, by their President and Secretary, signed and delivered this Contract, at the City of Raleigh, this _____ day of _____ 185_.

_____ PRESIDENT

_____ SECRETARY

This policy issued in 1855 provided coverage if the following conditions were met: the slave could not be removed from the state without the consent of the company and could not be covered by another insurance company while this coverage was in force. The company would not pay benefits in the event that "the said slave shall die for want of proper medical or personal attendance, or by means of any invasion, insurrection, riot or civil commotion, or of any military or usurped power, or by the hands of Justice; or shall die in open resistance to any authority or officer, legally constituted and appointed . . . or should said slave die whilst runaway from the service of the person or persons having the control and management of him or her, then this Policy shall be void, null, and of no effect." (Courtesy of the Joseph A. Linn Papers, Southern Historical Collection, University of North Carolina Library, Chapel Hill.)

Policy insuring "Sophia," a "House Girl," for $400. Signed January 15, 1855, in Greensborough, North Carolina. (Courtesy of the Joseph A. Linn Papers, Southern Historical Collection, University of North Carolina Library, Chapel Hill.)

For the sum of one dollar Joseph A. Linn in 1857 transferred his interest in an insurance policy on the life of a slave to John W. and Anderson Ellis. Slaves were often used as currency in land transactions, and sometimes used as collateral. (Courtesy of the Joseph A. Linn Papers, Southern Historical Collection, University of North Carolina Library, Chapel Hill.)

UNDER DECREE IN EQUITY.

SANDERS vs. SANDERS, et al.

On *Tuesday, the 11th January, 1859,* will be sold at the *Court House, in Charleston, at 12 o'clock, M.,* under direction of James W. Gray, Master in Equity, the following Slaves.

TERMS.—One-third Cash; balance in one, two and three years, secured by bonds and mortgages with approved personal security. Purchaser to pay for Papers.

	NAMES.	AGE.		NAMES.	AGE.
	1 London,	55 yrs.		52 Jacob	55 yrs.
	2 Nelly,	50		53 Mary	45
	3 Dick,	15		54 Emma,	21
4—	4 Rosy,	4		55 Rose	15
				56 Aelie	18
	5 Cuffy,	35		57 Simon	13
2—	6 Becker,	19		58 Francis	6
			8—59	Mary	3
	7 Caroline,	29			
	8 Martha,	4		60 Hardtimes	70
	9 Bull or Frederick,	12		61 Sary,	30
4—10	Infant,	9 ms.	3—62	Anne,	18
	11 Charity,	30 yrs.		63 Old Peter	70
	12 Susan,	17	2—64	Old Nancy	60
	13 Floride,	2			
4—14	Infant,	6 ms.		65 Old Hester	68
				66 Maggy	40
	15 Ned,	60 yrs.		67 Edward,	19
	16 Silvy,	35		68 Susan	17
3—17	Frank,	11		69 Robert	13
				70 Martha	7
	18 Easton,	3	7—71	Sarah	2
	19 Infant,	3 ms.			
	20 Billy,	68 yrs.		72 Peter	28
	21 Lucy,	50		73 Venus	25
	22 Binah,	14		74 Henry	8
	23 Phillis,	12		75 Hamilton	4
7—24	Jack,	11	5—76	Cornelia	1
1—25	Thomas,	26		77 Lydy	25
			2—78	Hannah	6 ms.
1—26	Toney,	30			
				79 Hannah	30 yrs.
	27 Becky,	30		80 Nero	10
	28 Sammy,	5		81 Rachel	7
	29 Fed,	3		82 August	4
4—30	Infant,	7 ms.		32 Henry	2
			6—84	Infant	1 mh.
1—31	Isaac,	30			
			1—85	Old Frank,	60 yrs.
1—32	Moses,	25			
			1—86	Toney	30
1—33	Morris,	21			
				87 Jake,	35
	34 Billy,	45		88 Eliza	30
	35 Hagar,	50		89 Pleasant	12
	36 Joe,	35		90 Sukey	10
	37 William,	20		91 Amanda	8
5—38	Rose,	15	6—92	Catharine	3
	39 Martha	70	1—93	David	36
	40 Nancy	45			
	41 Rachel,	22	1—94	Jim	39
	42 Ben,	16			
5—43	Lot	10	1—95	Binah,	60
	44 Betty,	25	1—96	March	40
2—45	Plymouth,	2			
			1—97	Bob	35
	46 London,	26			
	47 Grace,	22	1—98	Sarah	10
3—48	Harriet	2			
			1—99	Harriet	14
	49 Hester	25			
	50 Amos	21			
3—51	Elsey	5			

(Town Negroes.)

Handbill announcing sale of slaves, grouped by family, on January 11, 1859. (Courtesy of the South Carolina Historical Society. Major Hutson Lee Papers.)

	Name.	Age.	Qualification.		Name.	Age.	Qualification.
780	114 John Bascomb	40	Good carter	660	137 Henry,	45	Good patroon, blem. 1 eye
110	115 Will,	50	Laborer, ruptured	740	138 Gibby,	45	Good boat hand
530	116 Quamina,	40	Good laborer		139 Jacob,	45	Good boat hand
1000	117 David,	25	Prime laborer		140 George,	50	Boat hand
850	118 Charles,	50	Prime engineer		141 Prince,	55	Boat hand
1600	119 William,	28	Prime & faithful engineer		142 Cudjoe,	40	Cooper, ruptured
1050	120 Jim,	47	Tight bbl. cooper, slight defect in one finger		143 Adam,	55	Full task cooper, defect in one eye
J L							
1525	121 Richard,	40	Prime cooper		144 John Lewis,	40	Cooper, lines barrels, complains
1875	122 David,	35	Very prime cooper		145 Frank,	55	Cooper, lines barrels, defect in one eye
1500	123 Washington,	30	Prime cooper				
1120	124 Chance,	40	Prime cooper		146 Peter,	50	Prime cooper
	125 Gibby,	35	" "	J L	147 Paul,	60	Cooper
	126 Phillip,	33	" " cataract in 1 eye (brothers)				
					148 Marlboro',	60	Full task cooper, ruptur'd
1250	127 Samuel,	35	Prime cooper		149 Isaac,	65	Cooper, invalid
825	128 Sam,	50	Prime cooper, small lump on arm		150 Jack,	60	Good gardener
1200	129 William,	35	Prime cooper		151 Tom Huger	65	Laborer
T							
1600	130 June,	30	Prime cooper		152 Tom P.,	60	Laborer & painter, rupt'd
1100	131 Andrew,	35	Prime cooper		153 Sam,	55	Laborer, ruptured
B							
1675	132 Sancho	30	Prime cooper		154 Hannibal,	55	Laborer, ruptured
1150	133 Joseph,	30	Prime cooper		155 Aaron,	50	Laborer, sore leg
480	134 June,	50	Excellent Blacksmith		156 Jack,	65	Laborer
1100	135 Edward,	30	Prime laborer		157 Joe,	65	Laborer, unsound
JL							
800	136 Jeoffery,	45	Confidential patroon		158 Tom,	80	

4800
4850
780
1850
4500
2980
1760
1360
7140
2600

A handbill and inventory of slaves from Africa sold at public auction in Charleston. Information provided to prospective buyers included the name, age, skill, and disability—if any—of the slave. This lot was made up of 158 blacks. Amounts paid are noted on the left. As shown, the younger and skilled slaves brought the highest prices. (Courtesy of the South Carolina Historical Society, Major Hutson Lee Papers.)

KNOW ALL MEN BY THESE PRESENTS, That

I, Edward W. Mikell of the City of Charleston in the State aforesaid

for and in consideration of the sum of *One Thousand, six hundred and fifty Dollars*

to *me* in hand paid, at and before the sealing and delivery of these Presents,

by Charles Inglesby of the City and State aforesaid

(the receipt whereof *I* do hereby acknowledge) have bargained and sold, and by these presents do bargain, sell and deliver to the said *Charles Inglesby*

One Negro slave named Binah together with all the future issue and increase of said slave, — warranted sound

TO HAVE AND TO HOLD the said *slave Binah with her future issue and increase*

unto the said *Charles Inglesby his*

Executors, Administrators, and Assigns: to *his* and *their* only proper use and behoof forever. And *I* the said *Edward Wilkin-*
von Mikell my

Executors and Administrators, the said bargained premises, unto the said

Charles Inglesby his

Executors, Administrators and Assigns, from and against all persons, shall and will WARRANT and FOREVER DEFEND by these Presents.

In Witness Whereof, *I* have hereunto set *my* Hand and Seal dated at *Charleston* on the *twenty first* day of *March* in the year of our Lord one thousand eight hundred and *sixty one* and in the *first* year of the Independence of the ~~United States of America~~ *Confederated States of America*

SEALED AND DELIVERED IN THE PRESENCE OF }

Peleg S.C. Stone
John Squeeglfortin

Edward W. Mikell [L.S.]
Edward. W. Mikell.

As late as 1861, female slaves of childbearing age still commanded high prices. "In the first year of the Independence of the Confederate States of America," Edward W. Mikell of Charleston sold "one Negro slave named Binah together with all the future issue and increase of said slave" for $1650. (Courtesy of the South Carolina Historical Society, Major Hutson Lee Papers.)

Examinations of slaves Pompey, Edwin, and Frank, in relation to Denmark Vesey's slave insurrection in 1822. This report was an enclosure that accompanied Governor Thomas Bennett's message to the General Assembly of South Carolina concerning the famous revolt. (Courtesy of the South Carolina Department of Archives and History.)

On July 18, 1822, the death sentence was pronounced on those slaves captured and brought to trial following Denmark Vesey's slave insurrection. Among them was Denmark Vesey's brother Sandy. (Courtesy of the South Carolina Department of Archives and History.)

List of the fifty-five whites murdered during Nat Turner's revolt at Southampton, Virginia, on August 22, 1831. (Courtesy of the Swem Library, The College of William and Mary, Blow Family Scrapbook.)

List of the Negroes condemned & executed in Southampton

Names of Slaves.	Owners Names.	Time of Execution.	
Daniel	Richard Porter	5th Septr 1831.	
Jack	Caty Whitehead	12th " "	✪
Andrew	do	" " " "	✪
Moses	Thomas Barrow	5 " " "	
Davy	Elizabeth Turner	12 " " "	
Curtis	Thomas Ridley	" " " "	
Stephen	do	" " " "	
Isaac	George H. Charlton	20 " "	+
Mark	Joseph Travis	9 " "	
Sam	Nathl Francis	" " "	
Nelson	Jacob Williams	" do "	
Davy	Levi Waller	" 13 "	
Nat	Edd Turners Estate	" " "	
Jack	William Reese	12 " "	
Dred	Nathl Francis	" " "	
Nathan	Benjn Blunt	" " "	
Tom			
Nathan	Nathl Francis	20th "	+
Davy			
Hardy			
Isham	Benjn Edwards	" "	+

✪ Removed to Richmond, punishment Transportation

+ Recommended to Mercy.

"List of the Negroes condemned & executed in Southampton" in September 1831, following Nat Turner's revolt. (Courtesy of the Swem Library, The College of William and Mary, Blow Family Scrapbook.)

Fourteen days after Nat Turner's Southampton insurrection, William Campbell of Norfolk, Virginia, wrote to his friend Colonel Baldwin in Charleston, Massachusetts. The letter reports the feelings of the people in the surrounding countryside. Campbell writes: " . . . Our dining room table is much reduced. . . . There is no fun at table now, but our meals are tucked in with dispatch and with silence of a funeral meeting. . . . The whites murdered amount to fifty-eight – Excitement and apprehension exists all over the country, and here as much as any place. . . .   There was a large force on the guard last night and patrols all over the neighbouring country. . . .   I cannot think the Blacks so stupid as to expect any success in the present prepared state of the country. – Most of what we hear is groundless – all exaggerated. – I have not the slightest apprehension for the safety of the Whites. . . . (Courtesy of the University of Virginia Library, Manuscript Division.)

(continued on next page)

The whites murdered amount to fifty eight – Excitement and apprehension exists all over the Country, and here as much as any place. Yesterday morning eleven of Richd Drummonds' negros were apprehended and committed for trial, on the evidence of a young lad who stated that an insurrection was to take place today in Norfolk when the people were in the different churches – These were to be surrounded and the occupants destroyed – at same time the work of destruction by fire and sword was to go on all over the town. – Mr Drummonds' overseer says his negros had excited suspicion, and under the fear of punishment this youth gave this information – that is, the overseer. threatned him with chastisement if he did not disclose something which he believed was going amongst the gang. There was a large force on Guard last night and Patrols all over the neigh:bouring country. – Another of Mr Drummonds' men was apprehended about him last night under the following ci:-

:=cuated. – To say as much to some hot headed – & perhaps may say fearful people here would expose one to the risk of a quarrel – I have not the slightest apprehension for the safety of the Whites – I hope Mrs Baldwin will, have no apprehension of the kind to prevent her coming with you, or to make her uncomfortable if you come alone. – Pray offer her my compliments & remembrances

I send you a sheet of Caricatures to make up for a dull letter. – Believe me always,

My dear Sir
truly yours
Wm Campbell

"La Amistad," a watercolor by an unidentified artist. This painting descended in the Baldwin family and may have belonged to Roger Sherman Baldwin. The smaller vessel is the U.S. Brig *Washington*. In the foreground, Africans are shown trading. (Courtesy of the New Haven Colony Historical Society.)

Joseph Cinqué, a member of the Mendi people, Sierra Leone, and leader of the *Amistad* mutiny in 1839. Engraving by Sartain, after the 1840 painting by Nathaniel Jocelyn, owned by the New Haven Colony Historical Society. "What a master spirit is his . . ./What a soul for the tyrant/To crush down in bondage."/—John Greenleaf Whittier. (Courtesy of the National Portrait Gallery, Smithsonian Institution.)

John Quincy Adams. Daguerreotype, 1843. (Courtesy of The Metropolitan Museum of Art. Gift of I. N. Phelps Stokes.)

Roger S. Baldwin Esqr. New Haven

Washington Tuesday 9. March 1841. noon

Dear Sir

The decision of the Supreme Court in the case of the Amistad has this moment been delivered by judge Story. The Captives are free.

The decision of the District Court placing them at the disposal of the President of the United States to be sent to Africa is reversed. They are to be discharged as free. The rest of the decision of the Courts below including Lieutenant Gedney's claim for salvage, affirmed.

I requested the Clerk Mr Carroll, to transmit the order of the Court to the Marshal as soon as possible — He says it cannot be issued till after the Court rises to-morrow.

Yours in great haste and great joy.

J. Q. Adams.

On March 9, 1841, John Quincy Adams wrote to Roger Sherman Baldwin, an abolitionist who had been instrumental in securing legal counsel for the *Amistad* captives. Adams wrote, ''The decision of the Supreme Court in the case of the Amistad has this moment been delivered by judge Strong. The captives are free.'' (Courtesy of the Baldwin Family Papers, Yale University Library.)

The *Amistad* affair became a *cause célèbre* of the abolitionist movement. William H. Townsend drew the life portraits of more than twenty of the captives. These were later reproduced as wax figures and exhibited by abolitionists on speaking tours. At the conclusion of the case, the abolitionist Lewis Tappan and the American Missionary Association were instrumental in arranging for the return of Cinqué and his men to Sierra Leone in West Africa.

(Courtesy of the Beinecke Rare Book and Manuscript Library, Yale University.)

140

For the sum of "ten hundred Dollars, lawful money of the United States," Dred Scott (who made his mark) applied for and received a license from the County Court of Saint Louis "to reside in the State of Missouri." The license (ca. 1858) assured his good behavior and conduct. (Courtesy of the Missouri Historical Society.)

Fugitive Slave Bill.

As passed by the Senate and House of Representatives, Sept. 12, 1850, and approved September 18, 1850, by President FILLMORE.

AN ACT to amend, and supplementary to the act entitled, "An act respecting fugitives from justice, and persons escaping from the service of their masters," approved, Feb. 12, 1793.

SECTION 1. That persons who have been or may hereafter be, appointed Commissioners in virtue of any act of Congress, by the Circuit Courts of the United States, and who in consequence of such appointments, are authorised to exercise the powers that a *justice of the peace or other magistrate* of any of the United States may exercise in respect to offenders for any crime or offence against the United States, by arresting, imprisoning, or bailing the same under and by virtue of the thirty-third section of the act of the 24th of September, 1789, entitled "An act to establish Judicial Courts of the United States," shall be and are hereby *authorized and required to exercise and discharge all the powers and duties conferred by this act.*

SEC. 2. And be it further enacted, That the Superior Court of *each organized territory* of the United States, shall have the same power to appoint commissioners to take acknowledgements of bail and affidavits, and to take depositions of witnesses in civil causes which is now possessed by the Circuit Courts of the United States; all commissioners who shall be appointed for such purposes by the Superior Court of *any organized territory* of the United States, shall possess all the powers and exercise all the duties conferred by law upon the commissioners appointed by the Circuit Court of the United States for similar purposes, and shall moreover exercise and discharge all the powers and duties conferred by this act.

SEC. 3. And be it further enacted, That the circuit courts of the United States and the superior courts of each organized territory of the United States, shall, from time to time, *enlarge the number of commissioners, with a view to afford reasonable facilities to reclaim fugitives from labor*, and to the discharge of the duties imposed by this act.

SEC. 4. And be it further enacted, That the commissioners above named shall have concurrent jurisdiction with the Judges of the Circuit and District Courts of the United States, in their respective circuits and districts within the several States, and the judges of the superior courts of the territories, severally and collectively, in term time and vacation; and shall grant certificates to such claimants, upon *satisfactory proof* being made with *authority to take and remove such fugitives from service or labor*, under the restrictions herein contained, to the State or territory from which such persons may have escaped or fled.

SEC. 5. And be it further enacted, That it shall be the duty of all marshals and deputy marshals to obey and execute all warrants and precepts issued under the provisions of this act, when to them directed; and should any marshal or deputy marshal *refuse* to receive such warrant or other process, when tendered, or use all proper means diligently to execute the same, he shall on conviction thereof, be *fined in the sum of ONE THOUSAND DOLLARS to the use of such claimant* on motion of such claimant, by the circuit or district court of the district of such marshal; and after arrest of such fugitive by such marshal or his deputy, or whilst at any time in his custody under the provisions of this act, should such fugitive escape, *whether* WITH OR WITHOUT THE ASSENT OF SUCH MARSHAL OR HIS DEPUTY, such marshal shall be liable on his official bond to be prosecuted for the benefit of such claimant, for the *full value* of the service or labor of said fugitive in the State, territory or district whence he escaped; and the better to enable the said commissioners when thus appointed, to execute their duties faithfully and efficiently; in conformity with the requirements of the Constitution of the United States and of this act, they are hereby authorized and empowered, *within their counties* respectively to appoint in writing under hands *any one or more suitable persons* from time to time, to execute all such warrants and other process as may be issued by them in the lawful performance of their respective duties, with authority to such commissioners or the person to be appointed by them to execute process as aforesaid, to summon and CALL TO THEIR AID THE BY-STANDERS, or *posse comitatus* of the proper county, when necessary to insure a faithful observance of the clause of the constitution referred to, in conformity with the provisions of this act—AND ALL GOOD CITIZENS ARE HEREBY COMMANDED TO AID AND ASSIST IN THE PROMPT AND EFFICIENT EXECUTION OF THIS WHENEVER THEIR SERVICES MAY BE REQUIRED as aforesaid for that purpose; and said warrants shall run and be executed by said officers anywhere in the State, within which they are executed.

SEC. 6. And be it further enacted, That when a person held to service or labor in any State or territory of the United States, *has heretofore or shall hereafter* escape into another State or territory of the United States, the person or persons to whom such services or labor may be due, or his, her or their agent or attorney, duly authorized, by power of attorney, in writing acknowledged and certified under the seal of some legal officer of court of the State or territory in which the same may be executed, may pursue and reclaim such fugitive person, either by procuring a warrant from some of the courts, judges or commissioners aforesaid, of the proper circuit, district or county for the apprehension of such fugitive from service or labor, or by seizing and arresting such fugitive, where the same can be done *without process*, and by taking or causing such person to be taken, forthwith before such court, judge or commissioner, whose duty it shall be to hear and determine the case of such claimant *in a* SUMMARY MANNER; and upon *satisfactory proof* being made, by *deposition or affidavit*, in writing, to be taken and certified by such court, judge or commissioner, or by *other satisfactory testimony*, duly taken and certified by some court, magistrate, justice of the peace, or other legal officer authorized to administer an oath and take depositions under the laws of the State or territory from which such person owing service or labor may have escaped, with a certificate of such magistracy or other authority, as aforesaid, with the seal of the proper court or officer thereto attached, which seal shall be sufficient to establish the competency of the proof, and with proof also by affidavit, of the *identity* of the person whose service or labor is said to be due as aforesaid, that the person so arrested does in fact owe service or labor to the person or persons claiming him or her, in the State or territory from which such fugitive may have escaped, as aforesaid, and that said person escaped, to make out and deliver to such claimant, his or her agent or attorney, a *certificate* setting forth the substantial facts as to the service or labor due from each fugitive to the claimant, and of his or her escape from the State or territory in which such service or labor was due, to the State or territory in which he or she was arrested, *with authority to such claimant or his or her agent or attorney, to use such reasonable force and restraint as may be necessary*, under the circumstances of the case, to take and remove such fugitive person back to the State or territory from whence he or she may have escaped as aforesaid. IN NO TRIAL OR HEARING UNDER THIS ACT SHALL TESTIMONY OF SUCH ALLEGED FUGITIVE BE ADMITTED IN EVIDENCE; and *the certificates in this and the first section mentioned* SHALL BE CONCLUSIVE OF THE RIGHT OF THE PERSON OR PERSONS IN WHOSE FAVOR GRANTED, *to remove such fugitive to the State or territory from which he escaped, and shall prevent all molestation of said person or persons by any process issued by any court, judge, magistrate or other person whomsoever.*

SEC. 7. And be it further enacted, That any person who shall knowingly or willingly obstruct, hinder or prevent such claimant, his agent or attorney, or *any person or persons*, lawfully assisting him, her or them, from arresting such fugitive from service or labor EITHER WITH *or* WITHOUT PROCESS as aforesaid; or shall rescue, or attempt to rescue such fugitive from service or labor, from the custody of such claimant, his or her agent or attorney, or other person or persons lawfully assisting as aforesaid when so arrested, pursuant to the authority herein given and declared; OR SHALL AID, ABET, OR ASSIST SUCH A PERSON SO OWING SERVICE OR LABOR AS AFORESAID, DIRECTLY OR INDIRECTLY TO ESCAPE from such claimant, his agent or attorney, or other person or persons legally authorized as aforesaid, or SHALL HARBOR or CONCEAL such fugitive, so as to prevent the discovery and arrest of such person, after notice or knowledge of the fact that such person was a fugitive from service or labor as aforesaid, shall, for either of said offences be subject to *a fine not exceeding* ONE THOUSAND DOLLARS *and* IMPRISONMENT NOT EXCEEDING SIX MONTHS, by indictment and conviction before the district court of the United States for the district in which such offence may have been committed, or before the proper court of criminal jurisdiction if committed within any one of the *organized territories* of the United States; *and shall, moreover, forfeit and pay by way of civil damages to the party injured by such illegal conduct, the sum of* ONE THOUSAND DOLLARS FOR EACH FUGITIVE SO LOST, as aforesaid, to be recovered by action for debt, in any of the district or territorial courts aforesaid, within whose jurisdiction the said offence may have been committed.

SEC. 8. And be it further enacted, That the marshals, their deputies, and the clerks of the said district and territorial courts, shall be paid for their services the like fees as may be allowed to them for similar services in other cases; and where such services are rendered exclusively in the arrest, custody and delivery of the fugitive to the claimant, his or her agent or attorney, or where such supposed fugitive may be discharged out of custody for want of sufficient proof as aforesaid, then such fees are to be paid in the whole by such claimant, his agent or attorney; and in all cases where the proceedings are before a commissioner, he shall be entitled to a fee of TEN DOLLARS in full for his services in each case, *upon the delivery of the said certificate to the claimant*, his or her agent or attorney; or a fee of FIVE DOLLARS *in cases where the proof shall not in the opinion of such commissioner, warrant such certificate and delivery*, inclusive of all services incident to such arrest and examination, to be paid, in either case, by the claimant, his or her agent or attorney. The person or persons authorized to execute the process to be issued by such commissioners for the arrest and detention of fugitives from service or labor, as aforesaid, shall also be entitled to a fee of *five dollars each* for said person he or they may arrest and take before any such commissioner as aforesaid, at the instance and request of such claimant, with such other fees as may be deemed reasonable by such commissioner for such additional services as may be necessarily performed by him or them; such as attending at the examination, keeping the fugitive in custody, and providing him with food and lodging during his detention, and until the final determination of such commissioner; and in general for performing such other duties as may be required by such claimant, his or her attorney or agent, or commissioner in the premises, such fees to be made up in conformity with the fees usually charged by the officers of the courts of justice within the proper district or county, as near as may be practicable, and paid by such claimants, their agents or attorneys, whether such supposed fugitives from service or labor, be ordered to be delivered to such claimants by the final determination of such commissioner or not.

SEC. 9. And be it further enacted, That upon affidavit made by the claimant of such fugitive, his agent or attorney, after such certificate has been issued, that he has reason to apprehend that *such fugitive will be rescued by force* from his or their possessions before he can be taken beyond the limits of the State in which the arrest is made, it shall be the duty of the officer making the arrest to *retain the fugitive in his custody, and to remove him to the State whence he fled*, and there to deliver him to said claimant, his agent or attorney. And to this end, the officer aforesaid is hereby AUTHORIZED AND REQUIRED TO EMPLOY SO MANY PERSONS AS HE MAY DEEM NECESSARY to overcome such force, and to retain them in his service so long as circumstances require. The said officer and his assistants, while so employed to receive the same compensation, and to be allowed the same expenses as are now allowed by law for transportation of criminals, to be certified by the judge of the district within which the arrest is made, and PAID OUT OF THE TREASURY OF THE UNITED STATES.

SEC. 10. And be it further enacted, That when any person held to service or labor in any State or Territory, or in the District of Columbia, shall escape therefrom, the party to whom such service or labor shall be due, his, her or their agent or attorney may apply to any court of record therein, or judge thereof in vacation, and make satisfactory proof to such court or judge in vacation, of the escape aforesaid, and that the person escaping owed service or labor to such party. Whereupon the court shall cause a record to be made of the matter as proved, and also a general description of the persons escaping with such convenient certainty as may be, and a transcript of such record authenticated by the attestation of clerk and seal of the said court being produced in any other State, Territory or District in which the person so escaping may be found, and being exhibited to any judge, commissioner or other officer authorized by the law of the United States to cause persons escaping from service or labor to be delivered up, *shall be held and taken to be full and conclusive evidence of escape, and that the service or labor of the person escaping is due to the party in such record mentioned.* And upon the production by the said party of other and further evidence, *if necessary either oral or by affidavit*, in addition to what is contained in the said record of the identity of the person escaping, *he or she shall be delivered up to the claimant.* And the said court, commissioner, judge or other person authorized by this act to grant certificates to claimants of fugitives, shall upon the production of the record and other evidences aforesaid, grant to such claimant a certificate of his right to take any such person identified and proved to be owing service or labor as aforesaid, which certificate shall authorize such claimaint to seize or arrest and transport such person, to the State or Territory from which he escaped. Provided,

That nothing herein contained shall be construed as requiring the production of a transcript of such record as evidence as aforesaid. But in its absence the claim shall be heard and determined upon other satisfactory proofs competent in law.

Approved, September 18, 1850.

MILLARD FILLMORE

THE BLACK LIST.

Total vote from free States in favor of the Fugitive Slave bill.

DEMOCRATS.—*Maine*—Messrs. Fuller, Gerry, Littlefield—3.

New Hampshire.—Messrs. **HIBBARD** and **PEASLEE**—2.

New York—Mr Walden—1.

New Jersey—Mr Wildrick—1.

Pennsylvania—Messrs. Dimmick, Job Mann, McLanahan, Robbins, Ross and James Thompson—6.

Ohio—Messrs. Hayland and Miller—2.

Indiana—Messrs. Albertson, William J. Brown, Dunham, Gorman, McDonald—5.

Illinois—Messrs. Bissel, T. L. Harris, McClernand, Richardson, Young—5.

Michigan—Mr A. W. Buel—1.

Iowa—Mr Leffler—1.

California—Mr Gilbert—1. Total 27.

WHIGS.—Messrs. Elliot, *of Mass.*; McGaughey, *of Ind.*; John L. Taylor, *of Ohio*—Total, 3.

Total Ayes from free states, 30.

Following the passage of the Fugitive Slave Law, it was estimated that some 50,000 fugitive slaves relocated north of the Mason-Dixon line. According to Frederick Douglass, "Under this law the oaths of any two villains—the capturer and the claimant—are sufficient to confine a free man to slavery for life." Railroad companies were required to post this notice and to inspect the freedom papers of all black passengers. Failure to do so exacted heavy fines and possible lawsuits from slave owners. (Courtesy of the National Museum of History and Technology, Smithsonian Institution.)

Placard written by the Reverend Theodore Parker, a militant abolitionist and supporter of John Brown. Parker was responsible for the printing and distribution of the poster by the Vigilance Committee of Boston after the passage of the Fugitive Slave Law in 1850. (Courtesy of the National Museum of History and Technology, Smithsonian Institution.)

Portrait of John Brown by David Bustill Bowser, 1858. (Courtesy of the National Park Service, Harper's Ferry National Park.)

The Bible used by John Brown while awaiting trial for the insurrection at Harper's Ferry. (Courtesy of the Chicago Historical Society.)

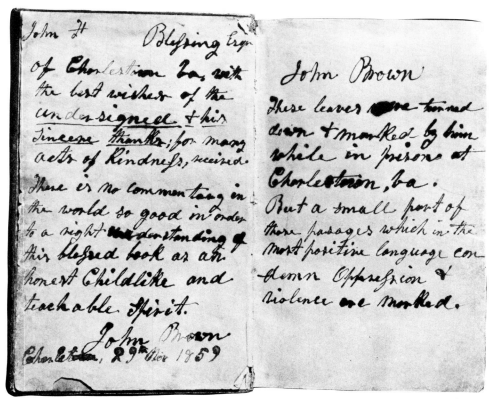

Pages from a Bible inscribed by John Brown in Charleston, Virginia (now West Virginia), on November 29, 1859. (Courtesy of the Chicago Historical Society.)

Gerrit Smith (1797-1874), a philanthropist from Petersboro, New York, helped finance the defense of the *Amistad* captives and John Brown's raid on the federal arsenal at Harper's Ferry. (Courtesy of Howard University, Moorland-Spingarn Research Center.)

On December 4, 1859, Palmer, Ackerman and Company received a letter signed by "A Southern Man" concerning "your man Williams." The writer threatens to tar-and-feather Williams, because " . . . *we will not tolerate . . . any man* who places himself upon an *equal* with a *negro . . .* we *no longer will have among us abolition emissaries."* After the warning of December 4, the company received the following letter. It reads in part: "We hope a warning already given you by one of our party will not be unheeded for we are fully determined and quite as *"able as determined"* to carry out *our threats* particularly in regards to that *scoundrel,* Williams, and it is our purpose soon to visit Saltsville with that determination . . . *look for us soon,* and expect the *execution of our threats* provided we find the mentioned party on the grounds. [Signed] *The Mountain Rangers."* (Courtesy of the Cornell University Libraries, Department of Manuscripts and University Archives.)

Office of PALMER, ACKERMAN & CO.,
Manufactures of Salt, Ground Plaster, &c., &c.

Saltville, Va. Nov 29 1859

Danl White Esq.
D. Sir
Herewith Enclosed please find articles of agreement signed by all the parties. You will observe the alterations. Mr Ackerman objected to having Deacon Spencer interest assigned to him and Mr Palmer and myself understood you to say that you was willing to have it assigned to you hence that alteration —

You will also observe that I have agreed for only two years from the first of January next including the business from its commencement. After looking at the business in all its details here and after having travelled with Mr Palmer more than a week in the Western markets down in Tennessee and also the eastern markets to some Extent east I made up my mind that I would not take and interest in it all but would return home for the reason that

write you giving you the particulars soon — I think the present Condition of the business looks very well

my Respectfully yours

C Comstock

P.S. This article of agreement is committed to your charge in behalf of all the parties with the understanding that either one is to have a copy at any time when Called for

C. Comstock

After the capture of the U. S. Arsenal at Harper's Ferry and John Brown's attempt to incite the slaves to revolt and strike for liberty, C. Comstock, a manager for the Palmer and Ackerman Salt Manufacturing Company at Saltsville, Virginia, made the following observation in a letter dated November 29, 1859: "It is rather a paculiar [sic] time here now the publick is much considerable excited on the Harpers Ferry affair and we anticipate some difficulty in getting Negroes to do our work the coming year. We cannot depend upon white labour. The hiring of niggers will take place about Christmas." (Courtesy of the Cornell University Libraries, Department of Manuscripts and University Archives.)

148

GAINING FREEDOM

As these documents attest, some slaves gained their freedom through the provisions of wills, manumissions, and self-purchase.

Freedom Documents

Freedom by will was not always immediate. Often the slave was required to serve yet another member of the family for a specified period of time, in accordance with the provisions of the will. Such was the case with William, Frank, Edd, and Philip, the slaves of John Cantine of Marble Town, Ulster County, New York. In his will dated November 5, 1803, Cantine ordered that his slaves serve his children. As each slave reached the age of twenty-eight, he would then be set free. (Courtesy of the Cornell University Libraries, Department of Manuscripts and University Archives.)

City of Philadelphia, ss.

BEFORE me the subscriber, one of the aldermen of the said city, person-
ally appeared *Samuel Winn a free black Man*
aged *twenty four* years or thereabouts, of the height of *five*
feet *five* inches, *dark Eyes black* complexion, *black curly* hair,
having *three flesh Moles on the right Side of his Neck*
and being duly *sworn* — on his solemn *Oath* saith,
that he does verily believe, from the accounts given him, he is of the age
aforesaid, and that he was born *on the Eastern Shore*
in the county of *Talbot* and state of *Maryland*
ALSO appeared, *John Smith a free black Man*
and being duly *sworn* on his solemn *Oath* saith,
that he knows and is well acquainted with the above named *Samuel*
Winn and that he believes the several
matters and things above set forth by him are true............And further these
deponents say not.

Sworn this *25* day of ⎱ *Samuel Winn*
December 18*10*. ⎰

Sam Shoemaker, *his*
Alderman *John + Smith*
Mark

An affidavit attesting to the legal status of "Samuel Winn [as] a free black man." Sworn to
before the alderman of Philadelphia on Christmas Day 1810, the affidavit was witnessed by
"John Smith a free black man," who made his mark. (Courtesy of Howard University,
Moorland-Spingarn Research Center.)

A petition to "The Hon. Speaker and Members of the House of Representatives of South ──→
Carolina" on behalf of the slave wife and children of Philip Stanislas Noisette, a white
botanist. The family was willed their freedom by their husband and father; the executors of
the estate petitioned that Noisette's wife and children be permitted to remain in the state as
"free people of colour." Philip Stanislas Noisette died in 1853. (Courtesy of the University of
South Carolina, The South Caroliniana Library.)

To the Honble
   The Speaker
      and
         Members of the House
of Representatives of South-Carolina. —

The Petition of the Children of Philip Stanislas
Noisette, late of Charleston, deceased. ———
   Showeth that their father, who died in
in the year 1835, was a practical Botanist,
and, during a long residence in this State,
contributed no little to develope the Natural
history of South-Carolina. that by his
Will he directed his Executors to take measures for the removal — l your Petitioners to

that they and their issue may be permitted
to remain in the State in the condition of
free persons of Color. ————————

        We recommend the Petitioners to the Le-
gislature as entirely worthy of their protection
        Danl F. Cos Weck
        S D Yeates.
        Chal E Kanapaup
        Jat Beghman
        A S John Laree
        James W Gray
        Jos. F. O'Hear
        Wm S Davidson.
        Moales Reith
        W S Fraser

151

The story of Peyton Polly clearly lends credence to the fears of Frederick Douglass and others who expressed grave concern about the Fugitive Slave Law. Beginning in 1850, with the kidnapping of Polly's seven children and nine-month-old grandchild, the case continued in the courts for eleven years, involved three states (Ohio, Kentucky, and Virginia) and the administrations of four governors of Ohio (Wood, Medill, Chase, and Dennison).

Because alleged fugitives did not have access to the courts and by provision of the law could not testify in their own behalf, the state of Ohio sought the children's return, charging that an ''outrage had been committed . . . against the dignity and sovereignty of the state.'' In his message to the General Assembly in 1852, Gov. Reuben Wood concluded with this thought: ''It is supposed that some time must intervene, before these suits can be brought to a close. . . . I ought, also, in justice to add, that, notwithstanding slavery is interwoven with all their institutions and civil relations south of the Ohio river, there is nevertheless to be found, noble and generous impulses in favor of the colored race, among a large portion of the people *where the right* to *freedom* is honestly *believed to exist*.'' (Courtesy of the Ohio Historical Society, Peyton Polly Papers.)

Louisville Oct 16th 1851

Hon Reuben Wood

Dear Sir

We take pleasure in informing you of the favorable issue of the suit of Peyton Polly for his freedom— The case was decided about one week ago, and to day we placed Peyton on board of the Steamboat Gen Pike bound for Cincinnati with a letter commending him to the care of Mess Campble Ellison &c of that City— He will, no dobt, be sent, with all convenient despatch, to his friends who, we understand, reside near Burlington Ohio—

Under the practice which prevails in our State, persons, suing for their freedom, are usually taken into the cus-tody of the court and hired out for such time as the suit may continue— the hirer giving bond with surity to treat them humanely and to use reasonable diligence in guarding against their escape— The requisition of such a bond—of course

he was managed—

We are pleased to be able to give you the further assurance that whilst there may be some wretches in Kentucky who would rob men even of their freedom the courts of this State are ready to do prompt and impar-tial justice—

Our charge for attention to the case is one hun-dred dollars—

Loughborough & Ballard

153

This testimony, dated April 9, 1853, is given on behalf of Henry J. Patterson, a free black moving from Raleigh, North Carolina, to Cleveland, Ohio. Among those bearing witness to his moral and upright character are the North Carolina secretary of state and George E. Badger, a member of the United States Senate (1846-1855). (Courtesy of Howard University, Moorland-Spingarn Research Center.)

154

(Jones)

Emancipation document of March 1859 executed by Ulysses S. Grant, liberating his "Negro man, William. . . ." (Courtesy of the Missouri Historical Society.)

The Still Family

Peter Still was born on Maryland's Eastern Shore, the son of Levin and Sidney Still. Sidney later changed her name to Charity to avoid detection and reenslavement. When Peter was a boy, his mother and two sisters escaped to freedom and joined the elder Levin in New Jersey. In retaliation, Peter and his older brother, Levin (junior), were sold to a Southern slave dealer, and his brother died. By the time his master died, Peter had married and was the father of three children. He was separated from his family and sold to a man who freed him in March 1851.

Peter Still was then reabducted and sold into slavery. He escaped to Philadelphia, where he was reunited with his mother Charity and a younger brother William. With their help, he began raising money to buy his wife and children from their owner. After thirty-six months of traveling in the northeastern states soliciting funds, Peter Still purchased his family's freedom for $6,000. In 1856, their story was told in a book entitled *The Kidnapped and Ransomed*.

Peter Still. (Illustration from William Still's *Underground Railroad*, 1872).

Charity Still, mother of William and Peter, who escaped twice from slavery. (Illustration from William Still's *Underground Railroad,* 1872.)

William Still, a Philadelphia agent of the Underground Railroad, was born after his parents were released from slavery. He played a prominent part in his brother Peter's eventual release from slavery. (Courtesy of the National Museum of History and Technology, Smithsonian Institution.)

From the Still family records, a list of the children born to Levin and Charity Still. (Courtesy of Rutgers, The State University of New Jersey, Archibald Stevens Alexander Library, Special Collections Department.)

Cover page of the *Still Family Memo Book,* about 1853-1854. (Courtesy of Rutgers, The State ⟶ University of New Jersey, Archibald Stevens Alexander Library, Special Collections Department.)

Pages from the *Memo Book* in which Peter Still recorded contributions made toward the ⟶ purchase of his wife's and children's freedom. (Courtesy of Rutgers, The State University of New Jersey, Archibald Stevens Alexander Library, Special Collections Department.)

Distance travelled by Peter Still
North East of Boston fare free
                                        receipt from Portland to Bath $1.—
    Boston to Lynn — 9 miles
        to Salem   5 — " —
        to Beverly   2 — " —
        to Newburypt 18 — " —
        to Portsmouth 20 — ? —
        to Biddeford — 35 — " —
        to Saco   2 — " —
        to Portland   13 — " —
        to Brunswick 27 — " —
        to Bath   9 — " —
                     ——————
                     140 miles
The fares when charged are
    Boston to Portland $3.00
    Portland to Bath   1.00
                            ——————
                             4.00
which would 48. going & returning but
he paid but $1.00 —
his whole expences out of Boston was $6.75
the above memo. made by
    Stephen Abbot Chase, Salem, Mass.
            at the request of Peter Still

Nancy Thayer
Sarah Burton
38 Federal street
Collected in Plymouth one
hundred dollars and in
Kingston 40 Dollars
            Justus Harlow

Collected in Fall River
One hundred and eighty
Dollars
            James M. Aldrich

Collected in Somerset
Twenty Dollars
            J. M. Aldrich.

Collected and paid Peter Still
in the city of Providence R.I. $250.00
            R. Conklin
    Providence Nov. 16th 1853
            D. B. Harris.

Collected and paid to Peter
Still in the City of New
York, from the friends
of Freedom, Ten Hundred
& Fifty Five Dollars
$1055 100/100   Thomas Foulke

Collected in Pittsfield,
Mass. & paid to Peter Still
one hundred & five
dollars & 92 cents.
            Samuel Harris
Pittsfield June 14, 1854

Collected and paid to
Peter Still in the City
of New Haven, Conn.
Three Hundred Dollars
July 7th   Jas. ?

Hartford Ct. July 31st 1854.
    Collected by Peter Still in the
city of Hartford Three Hundred Dollars
            Jos. R. Hawley.

In the Cars   .50

Middletown Aug 14th
Collected in the city of
Middletown. by Peter Still
One Hundred and Twenty Six
dollars, ?/100 — Esther Lewis

THE ABOLITIONISTS: Personalities and Documents

English and American abolitionists worked toward the same goal: the prohibition of the slave trade.

Wedgwood's Antislavery Medallion

Josiah Wedgwood (1730-1795), the famous English potter, was an active abolitionist. (Courtesy of the National Museum of History and Technology, Smithsonian Institution.)

Antislavery medallion created in 1778 by Josiah Wedgwood and given to Benjamin Franklin. (Courtesy of Dr. Lloyd E. Hawes.)

Benjamin Franklin's letter of acceptance of the Wedgwood medallion, dated May 15, 1787, to Josiah Wedgwood. (Courtesy of the Library of Congress, Prints and Photographs Division.)

THE

LIBERTY ALMANAC

FOR

1851.

AM I NOT A SISTER?

See the poor victim, torn from social life,
The shrieking babe, the agonizing wife!

New-York:

PUBLISHED BY THE AM. AND FOR. ANTI-SLAVERY SOCIETY:

WILLIAM HARNED, AGENT, NO. 61 JOHN STREET.

An American variation on Josiah Wedgwood's "Am I Not a Man and a Brother?" (Courtesy of The Library Company of Philadelphia.)

In this painting by Benjamin R. Haydon, English abolitionist Thomas Clarkson addresses the antislavery convention held in London in June 1840. (Courtesy of Howard University, Moorland-Spingarn Research Center.)

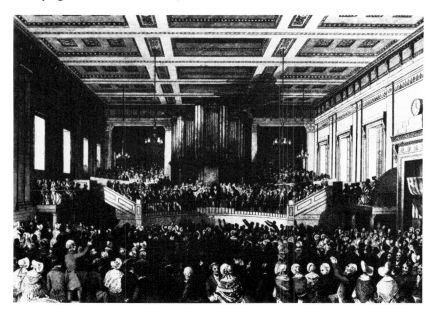

Exeter Hall, scene of the London World Anti-Slavery Conference in June 1840. The delegates listened to the fiery Daniel O'Connel. Charles L. Redmond, a black abolitionist, excluded himself from participation in protest against the conference's antifeminist rule that resulted in the refusal to seat women delegates. (Courtesy of the Library of Congress, Prints and Photographs Division.)

In 1838, thirty years after the passage by the British Parliament of the act to abolish the slave trade, Thomas Buxton wrote to Thomas Clarkson: " . . . The abolition of the Slave Trade by the English Parliament would cripple Slavery; & the abolition of Slavery would extinguish the Slave Trade.

I do not see why we should not attack the Monster, at both ends. Why should we wait, till Slavery is abolished? -before we attempt to stop such atrocities as exist in Africa & in the middle passage.

Are we to sit down and wait, till our Antislavery principles have worked their way, in Cuba & Brazil?

I fear that at least, this mode of proceeding, would cost us half a century, & that implies the sacrifice of twenty five millions of the human race, if my calculations be correct. [Signed] T. F. Buxton" (Courtesy of Howard University, Moorland-Spingarn Research Center.)

A letter from Granville Sharp to "W. Elford, Esq.," dated December 29, 1791. Granville Sharp wrote: "The Friends of this undertaking have neglected nothing in their power to open the Eyes of the Nation, and particularly to bring proof before the Legislature of the hateful Iniquities of this Traffick. A great impression has been made on the publick mind and, repulsed as we are, for the present, in that Quarter from which we had, as we conceived, well founded hopes of success, our chief dependence must remain on the virtue of the Community at large; and we cannot but hope that such a Combination of Talents as appeared in our favor, if supported by the voice of the people, will yet prevail over the confined Views and narrow prejudices of our opponents. . . ."(Courtesy of Howard University, Moorland-Spingarn Research Center.)

This portrait of Moses Brown (1738-1836), painted about 1898, is attributed to Henry E. Kinney and copied from a portrait of the elderly Brown painted by John Wesley Jarvis. Brown was a Rhode Island manufacturer and philanthropist. After the death of his wife in 1773, he became a Quaker and freed his slaves. Soon after, he helped found the Rhode Island Abolition Society. Following the Revolutionary War, he was among the first businessmen to become interested in cotton manufacturing.

On January 30, 1800, Brown wrote to Dwight Foster, a member of Congress from Massachusetts. Referring to his brother John, Moses Brown wrote: "He . . . has often appeared in Support of a Trade which his Love of Money and Anxiety to acquire it Long Since Drew his Brothers with him into Voyage in that Unrighteous Traffic, but happily they and I may say we Lived to Regret it, and Labour to have it Relinquished in this State; but my Brother John . . . has most unhapily as I think both for himself and others Continued Obstinately bent to Encourage the Trade. . . ." (Courtesy of The Rhode Island Historical Society.)

Silhouette of Moses Brown at age 93. Following his conversion to the Quaker religion, Brown became an active abolitionist and a friend of both Anthony Benezet and William Lloyd Garrison. (Courtesy of The Rhode Island Historical Society.)

Samuel Cornish (1790-1859), was an antislavery journalist who, with John B. Russwurm, started publishing *Freedom's Journal* in 1827. The first Afro-American newspaper, *Freedom's Journal* was a positive force in shaping social and economic policies and opinions in the black communities of America. (Courtesy of Howard University, Moorland-Spingarn Research Center.)

Samuel Ringgold Ward (1817-1864) escaped from slavery and became a writer and orator. Forced to flee to Canada because of his efforts on behalf of the abolitionist cause, he published his *Autobiography of a Fugitive Negro* in 1855. (Courtesy of Howard University, Moorland-Spingarn Research Center.)

William Wells Brown (1815-1884) was an escaped slave from Kentucky who joined Frederick Douglass on William Lloyd Garrison's antislavery lecture circuit. A pre-Civil War historian, Brown also served as an agent of the Underground Railroad. (Courtesy of Howard University, Moorland-Spingarn Research Center.)

A group of prominent abolitionists. Clockwise from the top, they are: John Quincy Adams, William Lloyd Garrison, Joshua R. Giddings, Cassius M. Clay, Benjamin Lundy, Owen Lovejoy, Gerrit Smith, William Cullen Bryant, and Henry Ward Beecher. In the middle, on top, is John Greenleaf Whittier; to the right is Charles Sumner and to the left is Wendell Phillips. (Courtesy of the Library of Congress, Prints and Photographs Division.)

A former slave who was active in the antislavery movement in Philadelphia, John Gloucester became pastor of the first African Presbyterian Church in 1807. (Courtesy of The Library Company of Philadelphia.)

Charles L. Reason (1818–?), the son of parents who fled the Haitian Revolution of 1793, was an educator, lecturer, poet, and an agent of the Underground Railroad. Reason was also a promoter of the national black convention movement. (Courtesy of Howard University, Moorland-Spingarn Research Center.)

Following the Revolutionary War, more and more people began to speak out, publish tracts and newspapers, and organize meetings in a concerted effort to end slavery.

AUCTION SALE OF SLAVES

Separation of Families! Plantation Scenes! Planters Residences and Slave Cabins! Negroes engaged in cultivating Cotton, Rice. Tobacco. Manufacturing Turpentine, &c. &c.

Together with the Thousand Incidents and Ills Slaves are heir to.

Habits and Customs of both Master and Slave—Mode of living—Implements of Torture, Places of Punishment, Hunting Fugitives with Blood Hounds, Terrific Encounter and Death of the Slave Hunter.

Residences of the poor whites of the South and their manner of living. &c., will be presented in

LIFE-LIKE SCENES!

To add to the interest of the Entertainment, the services of

ANTHONY BURNS

HAVE BEEN SECURED.

Mr. BURNS is the Fugitive who was remanded back to SLAVERY AND CHAINS, and whose arrest caused the *GREAT RIOT* in Boston, in June, 1854.

Mr. B., will present in truthful views, and describe Slavery from his own SAD EXPERIENCE.

FOR PARTICULARS SEE SMALL BILLS.

TICKETS 25 CENTS!

To be had at the usual places and at the door.

Children under 12 Years of Age, 15 Cents.

Doors open at 7 1-2 o'clk, P. M.,   Exhibition to commence at 8 o'clock.

This handbill advertises a performance by Anthony Burns, a fugitive slave whose attempted arrest and recapture resulted in ''the Great Riot'' in Boston in 1854. According to this notice, Burns's reenactment of ''life-like scenes'' will present ''the Thousand Incidents and Ills Slaves are heir to.'' (Courtesy of the National Museum of History and Technology, Smithsonian Institution.)

An illustration from a broadside published by abolitionists in 1836. The scene is a prison in Washington, D.C., where the sale of a free black is in progress to pay for his jail fees. Broadsides were an effective and popular form of propaganda for the abolitionist cause. (Courtesy of The New-York Historical Society.)

The British ship *Monkey* attacking the Spanish slave ship *Midas* on June 27, 1828, as an American vessel looks on. The British captured 369 slaves from the Spanish vessel, which had originally held 562; by the time the *Monkey* could land the slaves in Havana and free them, 78 more had died. (From W. E. F. Ward, *The Royal Navy and the Slavers*.)

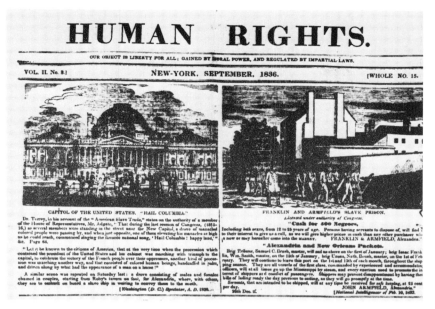

HUMAN RIGHTS.

OUR OBJECT IS LIBERTY FOR ALL; GAINED BY MORAL POWER, AND REGULATED BY IMPARTIAL LAWS.

VOL. II. No. 3.]   NEW-YORK, SEPTEMBER, 1836.   [WHOLE NO. 15.

CAPITOL OF THE UNITED STATES. "HAIL COLUMBIA."

FRANKLIN AND ARMFIELD'S SLAVE PRISON.

Washington, D.C., continued to be the focal point of attacks by abolitionists. In this issue of the abolitionist newspaper *Human Rights* in September 1836, the following notice was published: "Was committed to the prison of Washington Co., D.C., on the 19th day of May, 1834, as a runaway, a negro man, who calls himself *David Peck*. He is 5 feet 8 inches high. Had on, when committed, a check shirt, linen pantaloons, and straw hat. He *says he is free*, and belongs to Baltimore. The *owner* or *owners* are hereby requested to come forward, prove him and take him away, *or he will be sold for his prison and other expenses*, as the LAW DIRECTS./JAMES WILLIAMS,/Keeper of the Prison of Washington County,/District of Columbia." (Courtesy of The New York Public Library.)

Because of actions by the British Parliament, these Africans were rescued by the British vessel *Undine*. (Wood engraving published in *The Graphic*, June 7, 1884. Courtesy of the Library of Congress, Prints and Photographs Division.)

THE PRO-COLONIZATION MOVEMENT

Many people, both black and white, felt that the only solution to the racial problems in the United States was the resettlement of free blacks in a separate country.

"An act to authorize the President of the United States to permit the departure of Paul Cuffee, from the United States with a vessel & cargo for Sierra Leone, in Africa, and to return with a cargo." It is dated January 10, 1814. (Located in the National Archives and Record Service. Courtesy of the United States Senate.)

Cata logue of the famelies onboard the
Brig traveller going from America for Sierra Leon
in Africa Sailed 12 month 10 1815 [...]

Dersiy Locks 30 years old   William quinn about 60 years
Margret Locks 30 dito   Elizabeth quinn 56 dito
John Locks 11 do   Nancy quinn 17 dito
William Locks 9 d
Maryann Locke 7 do
Sarah Locks 5

Thomas Jervis 50 years old   Deter Willcox 40 years old
Judiath Jarvis 40 years old   Cloe willcox 34 dito
Judiath Jarvise junr 11 years old Eliza willcox 11 Dito
Thomas Jervis jr 9 years old   Sarah willcox 8 do
Alexander Jarvis 7 dito   Carolina willcox 6 do
Edward Jarvis 5 years old   Clarise Willcox 4 Do
Sarah an Jarvis 1½ Dito   Sussanah willcox 8 months

Samuel Hews 50 years old   Robart Rigsby 36 years old
[...] Hews 40 dito   Ann Rigsby 36 dito
Nancy Hews 14 dito   Catherinah Booath 12 dito
Samuel Hews 10 dito
Sarah Hews 6 dito   Samuel wilson 36 years old
Eliza ann Hews 1½ dito   Barbery wilson 28 about

Antona Servence 45 panda   Charles Calumbine 50 about
Elizabeth Serrence 45 do   Judiath Calumbine dito

A letter written in 1816 from Paul Cuffe to James Forten. Cuffe reports on having landed "all the passengers at Sierra Leone after a passage of 56 days, all in good health. The governor had granted them lands to farm on. . . ." Forten, a free black veteran of the Revolutionary War and War of 1812, originally supported Cuffe and the colonization movement. Later, Forten opposed colonization and convinced William Lloyd Garrison to do the same. (Courtesy of the City of New Bedford, Massachusetts, Free Public Library.)

Respected friend   westport 1 mo 8 1817

                    Robert Finly

thine of the 5 of December I have duly received but
not in time to answer thee at washington

        I observe from the printed petition in thy letter, the
the great great and laborous task you are engaged in
and my desires are that you may be guided by wisdoms
best means — I stand (as it were) in a low place and
am not abel to [see] fare; but blessed be god who hath
Created all things, and for his own glory they are and
were created; he is abel to make use of instruments
in such a way as he pleases; and may I be resined to his
holy will — the population of Sierra Leone 1811 was
about 2000 and about 1000 Subburbs & since that time
they have not been numbered, but I think the colony
from 1811 to 1815 hath much improved, they are entitled
to every privelege of free born citizens, and fill stations
in their courts — the soil in the colony of Sierra Leone
for cultivation are not flattering, but are very advant-
-ageously situated for a town, and a good ship harbour
the course of Africa abounds with rivers, the great
River gambia lieth about 350 miles N W of Sierra Leone
and the Island Buisse that lieth at the entrance of this
River are said to be very fertile, but are unhealthy for
the northern constitutions — there are another by the name
of Sherbour lieth about 50 Leagues S E of Sierra Leone

Letter written in 1817 from Paul Cuffe to Robert Finley in which he describes conditions in the colony of Sierra Leone: " . . . the population of Sierra Leone 1811 was about 2000 and about 1000 Subburbs & since that time they have not been numbered, but I think the colony from 1811 to 1815 hath much improved . . . " Robert Finley, a founder of the American Colonization Society, advocated colonization as a Christian act of charity. (Courtesy City of New Bedford, Massachusetts, Free Public Library.)

For the "Commonwealth":

Petition

To the Honorable, the Senate and House of Representatives in Congress assembled.

Whereas African slaves were, many years since, while we were yet colonies of Great-Britain, introduced among us to supply the lack of white labor, and increase the produce and exports of the British Plantations, whereby most of the States of this Union inherited, and many of them still retain, the institution of domestic slavery; and whereas some States, on the increase of the white population, finding the said institution to be a hindrance to their growth and prosperity, paralizing to their energies, most dangerous in war, and demoralizing in peace, have abolished the same, and since that time have far outstripped their sister states in which the said institution still subsists, in wealth, in population, in commerce, in development of their natural resources, and in whatever constitutes a nation great and prosperous; and whereas there are many States, especially in the middle section of this Union, which are believed no longer to need the assistance of slave labor, but whose interests and

In this undated petition, James B. Townsend proposes to the United States Congress: "That all vessels belonging to the United States, not necessarily employed in protecting our commerce may be used, under the direction of the Secretary of the Navy, in transporting to Africa such negro slaves as shall be voluntarily liberated and set free by their masters, . . . and such other negroes: or persons of color, already free, as shall voluntarily consent to such transportation.

"That appropriations may be made, from time to time, out of the surplus revenue of the United States, of such sums as Congress shall think reasonable to defray the necessary expenses in fitting out said negro-slaves [and] free negroes, . . . inasmuch as two separate races . . . can never commingle and coalesce." (Courtesy of the The Orlando Brown Papers, The Filson Club, Louisville, Kentucky.)

James Madison (1751-1836), the fourth president of the United States supported the work of the American Colonization Society, which he saw as the solution to the problem of slavery, the "dreadful calamity which has so long afflicted our country." (Courtesy of the Library of Congress, Prints and Photographs Division.)

This letter written in 1848 to Rev. N. M. Gordon, an agent for the American Colonization Society, from Robert MacNeilly, recommends the organization of Foreign and Domestic Mission Boards by the A. R. Synod of the South for the purpose of making them eligible to receive bequests of land or money. The intended use of the money was to provide continued support for their efforts to return free blacks to Africa. (Courtesy of the Special Collections, King Library North, University of Kentucky Libraries, Lexington.)

THE ANTI-COLONIZATION MOVEMENT

The colonization movement had its opponents. Many saw colonization as an evasion of the issues raised by slavery rather than a solution to them.

Mother Bethel African Methodist Episcopal Church, built in 1805. This structure replaced the blacksmith shop in which the Reverend Richard Allen founded the A.M.E. Church in the United States in 1794. Significantly, the rise of the black church signaled the beginning of more aggressive action on the part of free blacks to achieve self-determination. It was at Mother Bethel Church in January 1817 that 3,000 blacks, led by James Forten and the Reverends Richard Allen and Absalom Jones, voted not to support colonization. (Courtesy of the Mother Bethel A.M.E. Church Historical Commission.)

At a very numerous meeting of persons of colour, on the 16th instant, the following Resolutions were unanimously adopted:

Whereas, an address to the Citizens of Philadelphia and New-York, having been made through the medium of the public papers, by the agents of the American Society of Colonizing the Free People of Colour on the coast of Africa, which address is made, it is said in behalf of a number of people who are desirous of joining the projected Colony in Africa, and who have made application to the American Colonization Society for permission to be amongst its first colonists. But as a full and explicit expression of our sentiments and feelings relative to the proposed plan of Colonization, has already been submitted to the public, and as the views therein taken of the subject, were the result of cool and deliberate investigation; and as no circumstance has occurred since their adoption, to alter our opinion, but on the contrary, the reiterated expressions of some of the advocates of the measure, that it was foreign to their intentions to interfere with a species of property which they hold sacred, and by the recent attempt to introduce slavery in all its objectionable features, into the new states, and which has only been prevented by a small majority in the national Legislature, confirms us in the belief that any plan of Colonization without the American continent or Islands, will completely and permanently fix slavery in our common country. It is, therefore,

Resolved, That how clamorous soever a few obscure and dissatisfied strangers among us, may be in favour of being made Presidents, Governors and Principals, in Africa, there is but one sentiment among the respectable inhabitants of colour in this city and county, which is, that it meets their unanimous and decided disapprobation.

Resolved, That we are determined to have neither lot nor portion in a plan which we believe to be intended to perpetuate slavery in the United States. And it is, moreover,

Resolved, That the people of colour of Philadelphia, now enter and proclaim their solemn protest against the contemplated Colony on the shores of Africa, and against every measure that may have a tendency to convey an idea, that they give the project a single particle of countenance or encouragement.

JAMES FORTEN, Chairman.

RUSSEL PEROT, Sec'ry.

AFRICAN COLONIZATION.

In the following letter, which is a translation from the original put in our possession by Dr. Torrey, of Ballston, to whom it is addressed, it will be seen that the views of the American Colonization Society have excited the attention of President Boyer, of Hayti.—

American Daily Advertiser.

——PHILADELPHIA——

Thursday Morning, November 18, 1819.

MARRIED, at Woodbury, (N. J.) on Tuesday evening the 16th of November, by the Reverend Mr. Skinner, of Philadelphia, Mr. WILLIAM ALEXANDER TATEM, to Miss MARIA WEST, both of Woodbury.

On motion of JOHN HALLOWELL, Esq. Mr. JOSEPH S. PICKERING, was admitted to practice as an Attorney in the District Court for the City and County of Philadelphia.

LATE FROM MADRID.

Extract of a letter to the Editors of the Franklin Gazette, dated

"MADRID, September 13, 1819.

"Yesterday the duke of San Fernando was appointed secretary of state and despatch, answering to our secretary of state. Salmon who was acting as such, is made minister to Saxony. No person is designated to go to the United States. The duke San Fernando was selected, but was on his earnest solicitation excused by the king. The duke, who is connected by marriage with the reigning family, was apprehensive he should not, in the present posture of affairs, receive in America the attention his rank and royal connexion entitled him to expect. His character is said to be good.

"The fever among the troops in the vicinity of Cadiz still rages with violence.

"The treaty between Spain and Portugal for the delivery of Montevideo to the former, it is not yet agreed upon. It begins to be questioned whether Portugal means ever to make one."

Wilmington, (Del.) Nov. 17

DUEL.—Captain Robinson, on board of a sloop from this place, which was aground near Red Bank, opposite Fort Mifflin, on Sunday last, distinctly saw a Duel fought on the shore near him, by persons whom he had seen cross in boats from the Fort. At the first fire, one of the parties fell, and was conveyed across the river, mortally wounded, (as far as Capt. R. could judge from appearances.)

Probably the parties were officers, and the victim no doubt, has not only thrown away his own life, but may have wilfully added to the list of widows and orphans, and carried mourning and distress into many families of relatives, and severe regret into many more of friends. [Watchman.]

New York, November 16.

PICKPOCKET.—During the late Sessions, Antonio Manuel, was convicted of stealing a tobacco box, valued at 12 cents, taken from the pocket of an honest old man who is a retailer in the Bear Market. It appeared in evidence, that the tobacco box was generally

---

Newspaper account of resolutions opposing colonization, unanimously adopted on November 16, 1819, by the "People of Colour . . . City and County of Philadelphia." The meeting was chaired by James Forten. (Courtesy of The Library Company of Philadelphia.)

Liverpoolware jug with silhouette portrait of the Reverend Absalom Jones. Active in Philadelphia's civic and religious affairs, he organized along with Richard Allen, the Free African Society. He also organized independent black churches and founded an insurance company for blacks. (Courtesy of the National Portrait Gallery, Smithsonian Institution.)

THANKSGIVING SERMON.

PREACHED JANUARY 1, 1808,

In St. Thomas's, or the African Episcopal, Church Philadelphia:

ON ACCOUNT OF

THE ABOLITION

OF THE

AFRICAN SLAVE TRADE,

ON THAT DAY,

BY THE CONGRESS OF THE UNITED STATES

BY ABSALOM JONES,

RECTOR OF THE SAID CHURCH.

Sermon delivered by the Reverend Absalom Jones to celebrate the abolition of the African slave trade on January 1, 1808, as provided for by the United States Constitution. (Courtesy of the National Museum of History and Technology, Smithsonian Institution.)

Phillip A. Bell was one of the leaders, along with Samuel Ennals, who organized a mass meeting of blacks that was held in New York City on January 25, 1831, in opposition to the founding of a New York branch of the American Colonization Society. The group denounced the goals of the society and proclaimed that "the time must come when the Declaration of Independence will be felt in the heart, as well as uttered from the mouth. . . . This is our home, and this is our country. Beneath its sod lie the bones of our fathers; for it, some of them fought, bled, and died. Here we were born, and here we will die." (Published in *The Liberator,* February 12, 1831. Courtesy of Howard University, Moorland-Spingarn Research Center.)

Robert Purvis was among the influential participants and delegates in the National Negro Convention movement which was a strong force in America's black communities and provided a forum for addressing many significant issues. The Fifth Annual National Negro Convention met in Philadelphia in June of 1835. At this meeting, it was "Resolved, That the free people of colour are requested by this convention to petition those state legislatures that have adopted the Colonization Society, to abolish it. . . ." (Courtesy of Howard University, Moorland-Spingarn Research Center.)

MEMORIAL DISCOURSE;

BY

REV. HENRY HIGHLAND GARNET,

DELIVERED IN THE HALL OF THE HOUSE OF REPRESENTATIVES,

WASHINGTON CITY, D. C.

ON SABBATH, FEBRUARY 12, 1865.

WITH AN

INTRODUCTION,

BY

JAMES McCUNE SMITH, M. D.

PHILADELPHIA:
JOSEPH M. WILSON.
1865.

Henry Highland Garnet (1815-1882), an abolitionist, was elected secretary of the New York State Convention of Negroes in 1840. These state conventions of black people became important instruments of struggle before the Civil War. In 1843, Garnet issued his call to rebellion, "An Address to the Slaves of the United States." Garnet first opposed colonization efforts as a "fraudulent scheme to rob blacks of their citizenship." Influenced by Martin R. Delany, Garnet later became an emigrationist. The first black to speak in the House of Representatives, Garnet delivered his "Memorial Discourse" in celebration of the end of slavery. Garnet died while serving as the United States minister to Liberia. (Courtesy of Howard University, Moorland-Spingarn Research Center.)

Frederick Douglass (1817?-1895) was a leading abolitionist and an opponent of the colonization movement. (Courtesy of the National Portrait Gallery, Smithsonian Institution.)

Major Martin R. Delany was born in Virginia and educated in Pennsylvania where he was a student of medicine and dentistry. As a social activist, he became an emigrationist. His thoughts on the subject are expressed in *The Condition, Elevation, Emigration, and Destiny of the Colored People of the United States Politically Considered,* published in 1852. Between 1858 and 1861, he attempted to create a model community in the Niger Valley (East Africa), after which he redirected his efforts to the struggle of black's in America. Delany was commissioned an officer shortly before the end of the Civil War. (Courtesy of Howard University, Moorland-Spingarn Research Center.)

LIBERIA

Sponsored by the American Colonization Society, in 1820 the first black settlers arrived in the country they would call Liberia—Latin for *free man*.

Blacks from Arkansas awaiting transportation to Liberia at Mount Olivet Baptist Church in New York City. (Courtesy of the Library of Congress, Prints and Photographs Division.)

The U.S.S. Schooner *Alligator* by an unidentified artist (ca. 1860) was built at the Boston Navy Yard in 1820-21. The *Alligator* made her first trip to the West Coast of Africa in February 1821. Her orders were to capture vessels engaged in the slave trade. Then, she was to sail along the coast and select a site for the establishment of a colony for the captured slaves. The chosen site became Liberia. Between April 3 and October 4, 1821, the *Alligator* seized several slave ships, among them the schooners *Mathilde, l'Eliza,* and *Daphne.* (Courtesy of The Bailey Collection, The Mariner's Museum, Newport News, Virginia.)

Shoreline of Liberia. (Courtesy of Howard University, Moorland-Spingarn Research Center.)

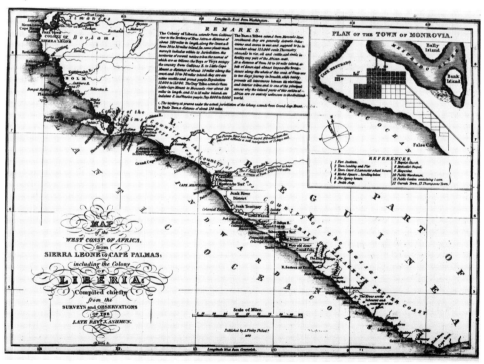

A "map of the West Coast of Africa from Sierra Leone to Cape Palmas: including the colony of Liberia: compiled chiefly from the surveys and observations of the late Rev. J. Ashmun." With it is a plan for the town of Monrovia. (From the *American Colonization Society Colonial Journal*, volume 6.)

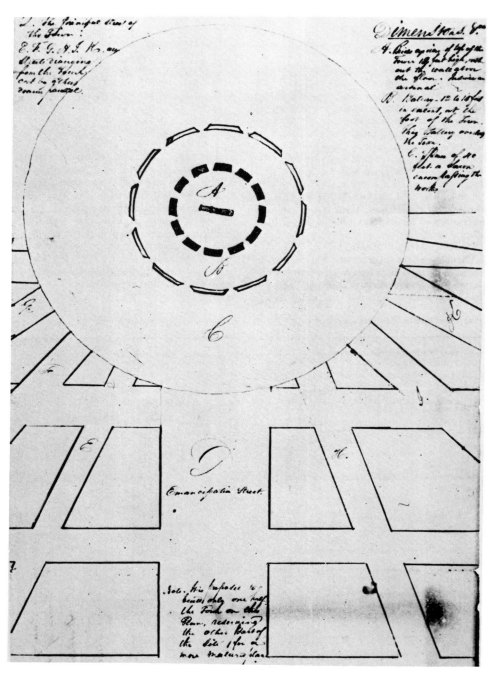

Cape Mesurado—present-day Monrovia—was the American Colonization Society's first settlement in Africa. This plan was probably drawn up by William Thornton, the architect for the United States Capitol and a member of the society's board of managers. The design (dated April 1823) calls for a tower and arsenal (A), a battery (B), and a lawn (C) that would be the focus of a number of converging streets, the most prominent being Emancipation Street. (Courtesy of the Library of Congress, Prints and Photographs Division.)

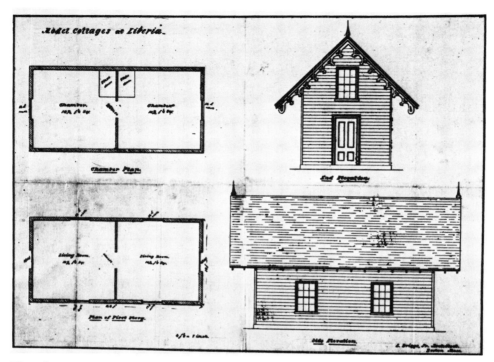

Plans for cottages for colonists, to be built in Liberia. (From the papers of the American Colonization Society, courtesy of the Library of Congress.)

A view of the colonial settlement at Cape Montserado [Mesurado]. (From the *American Colonization Society Colonial Journal,* volume I.)

House-building among the Vai people, the indigenous population in Liberia. (Courtesy of Howard University, Moorland-Spingarn Research Center.)

The view of Monrovia from Bushrod's Island, named for Bushrod Washington, a founding member of the American Colonization Society and a nephew of George Washington. (Courtesy of the Library of Congress, Prints and Photographs Division.)

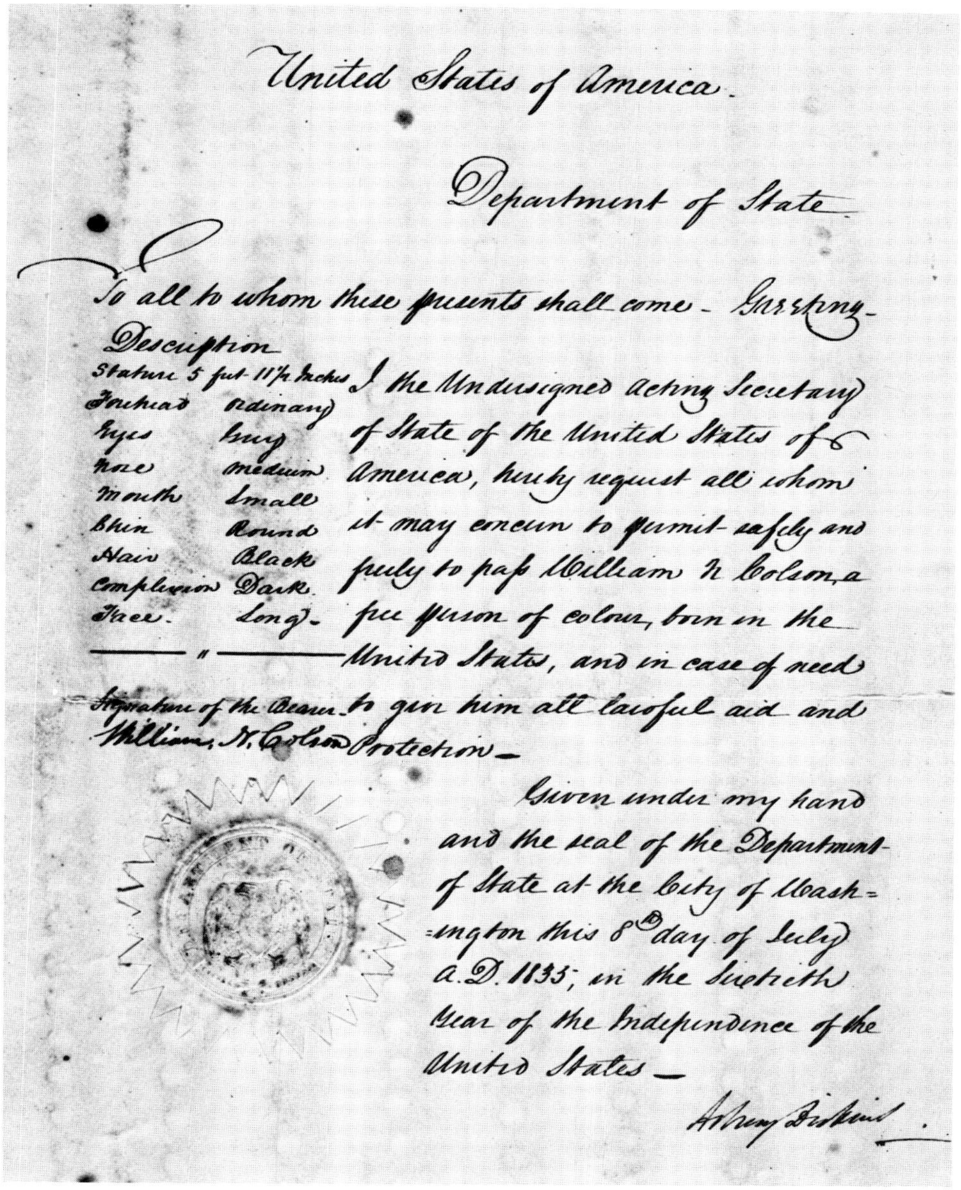

United States of America.

Department of State

To all to whom these presents shall come — Greeting —

Description

Stature 5 feet 11½ Inches
Forehead   ordinary
Eyes   gray
Nose   medium
Mouth   small
Chin   Round
Hair   Black
Complexion Dark.
Face   Long —

Signature of the Bearer

William N. Colson

I the Undersigned acting Secretary of State of the United States of America, hereby request all whom it may concern to permit safely and freely to pass William N Colson, a free person of colour, born in the United States, and in case of need to give him all lawful aid and Protection —

Given under my hand and the seal of the Department of State at the City of Washington this 8th day of July a.D. 1835; in the Sixtieth Year of the Independence of the United States —

Asbury Dickins.

Passport of William Colson, noting that he is "a free person of colour. . . ." (Courtesy of Mrs. Myra Colson Callis.)

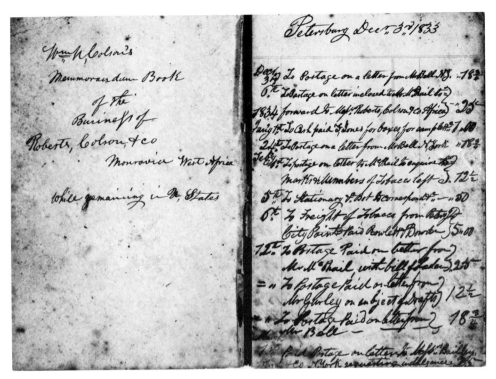

A page from "William Colson's Memorandum Book of the Business of Roberts, Colson, and Co. Monrovia, West Africa." Colson, an early Liberian businessman, was in partnership with Joseph Jenkins Roberts, the first president of the Republic of Liberia. (Courtesy of Mrs. Myra Colson Callis.)

The home of President Roberts in Monrovia, Liberia. (Courtesy of the Library of Congress, Prints and Photographs Division.)

Portrait of Joseph Jenkins Roberts by Thomas Wilcocks Sully. Born of slave parents in Petersburg, Virginia, Joseph Jenkins Roberts (1809-1876) was the first elected president of Liberia. (Courtesy of The Historical Society of Pennsylvania.)

Jane Roberts, widow of Joseph Jenkins Roberts, the first president of Liberia. This photograph was taken in 1905. (Courtesy of Howard University, Moorland-Spingarn Research Center.)

Ashmun Street, Monrovia, West Africa. Located on the street were a Methodist Episcopal Church, a Roman Catholic mission house, a monument to Joseph Jenkins Roberts, and the homes of many prominent Liberians, including Mrs. Joseph Jenkins Roberts. (Courtesy of the Library of Congress, Prints and Photographs Division.)

The *Mary Caroline Stevens*, a ship built in Baltimore in 1856 to carry blacks to Liberia. (Courtesy of the Maryland Historical Society, Baltimore.)

Maryland in Liberia, oil on canvas by John H. B. Latrobe, a president of the American Colonization Society. (Courtesy of the Maryland Historical Society, Baltimore.)

John B. Russwurm (1799-1851), a prominent figure in Liberia's early history, was the second black to receive a college degree in the United States. In 1827 he began editing the first black newspaper, *Freedom's Journal* (later *The Rights of All*). Although initially opposed to colonization, he later changed his mind and emigrated to Liberia. He founded the *Liberia Herald* and served as superintendent of schools. He was also governor of the African province of Maryland, which was later annexed to Liberia. (Courtesy of the New York Public Library: Astor, Lenox, and Tilden Foundations; Schomburg Center for Research in Black Culture.)

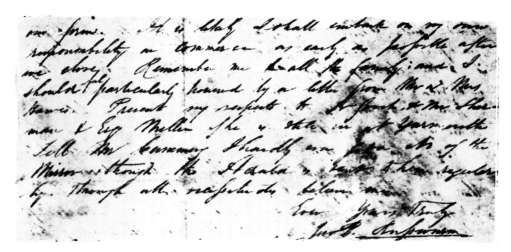

Letter written from Liberia by John B. Russwurm, dated March 31, 1834. About Liberia, he says: "The reports you see published in the U.S. are much exaggerated about its unhealthiness to those who merely come on & go off in the span of 6 or 9 months." Then he adds: "At present our coast is completely overrun with vessels of all nations—many engaged in the Slave Trade but a respectable number in fair trade." (Courtesy of The Tennessee State Library and Archives, Manuscript Section, John Sumner Russwurm Papers.)

Boston November 11. 1851.

Lehigh Coal & Navigation Co.   Dr.
2   To Donation account.
For a bequest of the late Jos. White
of Philadelphia of 100 shares in
said Comp.y Certif. No 3510. par
Value being $50. per share, the same
having been received from Mess.rs Rich.d
Richardson & John J. White, Ex.rs of
Josiah White's Estate,   ✓   5000.—

                    13.

4 2 Notes Receivable Dr To Donation %c
       For Rev.d Ralph Emerson D.D. note
       this date, on dem.d with interest   ✓   50.

                Jan.y 13. 1852.

6 2 Interest Dr   To Donation %c
       For balance of Interest %c   ✓   46 45

                    13.

2 3 Donation %c Dr   To Expense %c
       For balance of Expense %c , being
       the amount of Incidental Expenses
       during the year   ✓   208.01

A page from a *Journal . . . of Donations for Education in Liberia.* Among those contributing in Boston on November 11, 1851, was the Reverend Ralph Waldo Emerson. A poet and lecturer, Emerson began addressing abolitionist meetings about 1840. He supported the colonization movement, believing that "the [N]egro must elevate himself." (Courtesy of Harvard University, Baker Library.)

Alexander Crummell (1819-1898) was a graduate of Cambridge University. An Episcopal priest and missionary to Liberia for twenty years, he taught at Liberia College. Acknowledging that Harvard and Yale colleges had made "liberal donations of minerals and large gifts of books" to Liberia College, in a letter of 1862 to Joseph Henry, Secretary of the Smithsonian Institution, Crummell requested "the addition of the publications of the Smithsonian Institution to the collections already made for the Liberia College." (Letter in the Joseph Henry Papers, Smithsonian Institution.)

Signatures of faculty members of Liberia College. (Courtesy of the National Museum of History and Technology, Smithsonian Institution.)

Daniel Dashiel Warner was born free in Baltimore County, Maryland, in 1815. He emigrated to Liberia with his family in 1833. As a young man Warner entered government service, and in 1864 he was elected the third president of Liberia. (Courtesy of The Historical Society of Pennsylvania.)

Cape Palmas, Liberia. (Courtesy of the Library of Congress, Prints and Photographs Division.)

EPILOGUE: We the Children of Africa in This Land

Forget nothing but set everything in its rightful place: the glory of the six Ashanti Wars against Britain; the wisdom of the Fanti Confederation, the unity of Nigeria; the song of the Songhay and Hausa; the rebellion of the Mahdi and the hands of Ethiopia; the greatness of the Basuto and the fighting of the Chaka; the revenge of the Mutessa, and many other happenings and men; but above all–Africa, Mother of Man.

W. E. B. Du Bois
from *Africa Awake,* 1958

"A Ballad of Negro History"

There is so much to write about
In the Negro race.
On each page of history
Glows a dusky face.
Ancient Pharoahs come to mind
Away back in B.C.
Ethiopia's jeweled hand
Writes a scroll for me.
It was a black man bore the Cross
For Christ at Calvary.
There is so much to write about
In the Negro race.
Though now of Ghana's Empire
There remains no trace,
Once Africa's great cultures
Lighted Europe's dark
As Mandingo and Songhay
Cradled learning's ark
Before the Moors crossed into Spain
To leave their mark.
There is so much to write about
In the Negro race.
Ere the ships of slavery sailed
The seas of dark disgrace,
Once Antar added
Winged words to poetry's lore
And Juan Latino searched
The medieval heart's deep core –

All this before black men in chains
At Jamestown were put ashore.
There is so much to write about
In the Negro race,
So many thrilling stories
Time cannot erase:
Crispus Attuck's blow for freedom,
Denmark Vesey's, too.
Sojourner Truth, Fred Douglass,
And the heroes John Brown knew
Before the Union Armies gave
Black men proud uniforms of blue.
1863 – Emancipation!
The Negro race
Began its mighty struggle
For a rightful place . . .
There is so much to write about
To sing about, to shout about
In the Negro race!
On each page of history
America sees my face –
On each page of history
We leave a shining trace –
On each page of history
My race! My race! My race!

Attributed to Langston Hughes
1951

Most of these photographs were taken around the turn of the century on St. Helena Island off the coast of South Carolina. These pictures show in a simple, direct way, the persistence of the African heritage in the lives of black Americans. That heritage is still alive today and is part of the great story that is emerging, even now, out of Africa. (Photographs courtesy of The York W. Bailey Cultural Center, Penn Community Service, Inc. [St. Helena Island], Frogmore, South Carolina.)

202

204

LENDERS TO THE EXHIBITION AND CATALOGUE

Production of this exhibit and catalogue would have been impossible without the generous cooperation of the following institutions and individuals:

Bibliothèque Nationale, Paris, France

Mrs. Myra Colson Callis

The Chicago Historical Society

The Chicago Public Library

City of New Bedford, Massachusetts: Free Public Library

The College of William and Mary: Swem Library

Columbia University Libraries: George Arthur Plimpton Manuscript Collection

The Connecticut Historical Society

Cornell University Libraries: Department of Manuscripts and University Archives

Department of the Navy, Washington Navy Yard: Naval Historical Center

Disciples of Christ Historical Society, Nashville, Tennessee

Duke University, Durham, North Carolina: William R. Perkins Library, Manuscript Department

The Filson Club, Inc., Louisville, Kentucky

Georgia Department of Archives and History

Harvard University: Baker Library; The President and Fellows of Harvard College; The Peabody Museum

Dr. Lloyd E. Hawes

The Historical Society of Pennsylvania

Howard University: Moorland-Spingarn Research Center; Art Department

The Institute of Jamaica, West India Reference Library, Kingston, Jamaica

Mr. Reginald L. Jackson

John Street United Methodist Church, New York, New York

The Library Company of Philadelphia

The Library of Congress: Manuscript Division; Prints and Photographs Division

The Mariner's Museum, Newport News, Virginia: The Bailey Collection

Maryland Historical Society, Baltimore: Museum and Library of Maryland History

The Metropolitan Museum of Art: Division of Prints and Photographs; Michael C. Rockefeller Memorial Collection of Primitive Art (on loan from Nelson A. Rockefeller)

Mississippi State University: Mitchell Memorial Library

Missouri Historical Society

Mother Bethel African Methodist Episcopal Church, Philadelphia, Pennsylvania: Historical Commission

Museum of African Art, Washington, D.C.: Elisofon Archives

Museum of Fine Arts, Boston, Massachusetts

National Archives and Records Service with permission of the United States Senate

New Haven Colony Historical Society

The New-York Historical Society

The New York Public Library

The Ohio Historical Society

Old Dartmouth Historical Society, New Bedford, Massachusetts: Whaling Museum

Mr. Ted Pontiflet

The Rhode Island Historical Society

Rutgers, The State University of New Jersey: Archibald Stevens Alexander Library, Special Collections Department

The Rutherford B. Hayes Library, Fremont, Ohio

Mr. Fletcher A. Smith

Smithsonian Institution: Hirshhorn Museum and Sculpture Garden; National Museum of History and Technology; National Museum of Natural History; National Portrait Gallery

South Carolina Department of Archives and History

South Carolina Historical Society

State Historical Society of Wisconsin

The Tennessee State Library and Archives, Manuscript Section

United Presbyterian Church, Philadelphia, Pennsylvania: Department of History, Presbyterian Historical Society

United States Department of the Interior National Park Service: Harpers Ferry National Historical Park; Independence National Historical Park; American Museum of Immigration, Statue of Liberty National Monument

The University of Chicago, The Joseph Regenstein Library

University of Kentucky Libraries, Lexington: King Library, North, Special Collections

University of Missouri Library: Western Historical Manuscript Collection; State Historical Society Manuscripts

The University of North Carolina Library, Chapel Hill: Southern Historical Collection

University of South Carolina, The South Caroliniana Library

University of Virginia Library, Manuscript Department

The Western Reserve Historical Society, Cleveland, Ohio

Yale University: Roger Sherman Baldwin Papers and the Beinecke Rare Book and Manuscript Library

York W. Bailey Cultural Center, Penn Community Services, Inc. (Saint Helena Island), Frogmore, South Carolina

SELECTED BIBLIOGRAPHY

Primary Source Materials

In preparing the *Out of Africa* catalogue and exhibit, the Research Department of the Anacostia Neighborhood Museum has used selected documents from the following manuscript collections.

Atlanta. Georgia Department of Archives and History. Transcript – Negro Insurrection Trial, Johnson County, 1875.
Boston. Baker Library. Harvard University. An Account Book of the Spanish Royal Company, Cuba. (1752-1758)
    "Cash Book, Journal & Ledger of the Treasurer Trustees of Donations for Education in Liberia, Boston, 1850."
Chapel Hill. Manuscript Department and Southern Historical Collection. University of North Carolina Library.
    DeRosset Family Papers.
    Joseph A. Linn Papers.
    The Manumission Society Papers.
Charlottesville. Manuscripts Department. University of Virginia Library.
    William Campbell Letter.
    Conway Family Account Book.
    George E. Grymes Manager's Journal.
    R. T. Hubard Register of Slaves.
    Thomas Jefferson Papers. Farm Book.
    Samuel Whitcomb Papers.
Chicago. Chicago Historical Society.
    Richard D. Arnold Papers.
    Thomas Hart Benton Papers.
    John Payne Papers.
    Franklin Pierce Papers.
    Slavery Songs.
    Joseph Ward Papers.
Chicago. The Joseph Regenstein Library. The University of Chicago.
    Orator F. Cook Papers.
Columbia. Western Historical Manuscripts Collection. University of Missouri Library.
    Thomas Adams Smith Papers.
Columbia. South Carolina Department of Archives and History.
    Legislative and Executive Papers, 1782-1877.

Will of John Deas, November 26, 1790.
Will of Philip Stanislas Noisette, April 10, 1835.
Columbia. South Caroliniana Library. University of South Carolina.
David Ethan Frierson Papers.
Noisette Family Papers.
Columbus. Archives-Manuscripts Division. The Ohio Historical Society, Inc.
Peyton Polly Papers.
Concord. New Hampshire Historical Society.
Enoch Greenleafe Parrott Letters.
Durham [N.C.]. Duke University.
Tyre Glen Papers.
John Moore McCalla Papers.
Hartford. Connecticut Historical Society.
Letters Concerning Haiti.
Ithaca [N.Y.]. Department of Manuscripts & University Archives. Cornell University Libraries.
Sidney Ayres Papers.
Cantine Family Papers.
Civil War Pamphlets.
Vanderpoel Papers.
Ernest I. White Papers.
Lexington. Special Collections and Archives. University of Kentucky Libraries.
Gordon Family Papers.
Louisville [Ky.]. The Filson Club, Inc.
Orlando Brown Papers.
Madison. State Historical Society of Wisconsin.
Affidavit attesting to the freedom of Scipio Philips, April 26, 1811.
Bill to be entitled An act in relation to Warrantees on the sale of Slaves [Mississippi Legislature], December 1861.
Form of oath used when transferring slaves from state to state, dated November 1, 1778.
J. M. Winterbotham Papers.
Mississippi State. Mitchell Memorial Library. Mississippi State University.
Isaac Ross Estate Papers.
Nashville. Manuscript Section. The Tennessee State Library and Archives.
Chapman Family Papers.
Jacob McGavock Dickinson Papers.
John Sumner Russwurm Papers.
New Bedford. City of New Bedford, Massachusetts, Free Public Library.
Paul Cuffee Papers.
New Brunswick. Rutgers, The State University of New Jersey.
African Association of New Brunswick, New Jersey, Records.
Peter Still Collection.
New Haven [Conn.]. Beinecke Rare Book Library. Yale University.
Baldwin Family Papers.
Sketches of *Amistad* Captives.
New York. Columbia University in the City of New York.
George A. Plimpton Collection on Slavery.
Providence. The Rhode Island Historical Society.
Thomas Howland Manuscript Notes.
Saint Louis. Missouri Historical Society.
U. S. Grant Papers.
P. Dexter Tiffany Papers.

Washington, D.C.
The Library of Congress: Manuscript Division; Prints and Photographs Division; American Colonization Society Collection.
———. Moorland-Spingarn Research Center, Howard University: Charles Chapman Correspondence; Thomas Clarkson Correspondence; Charlotte Forten Grimke Diaries; Gerritt Smith Papers.
———. National Archives and Records Service: Senate Record Group 13A-B1.
———. Naval Historical Center, Washington Navy Yard: Department of the Navy Documents.
———. Smithsonian Institution: The Joseph Henry Papers; Smithsonian Archives.
Williamsburg. The College of William and Mary in Virginia.
Blow Family Papers.

Secondary Source Materials

Afro-American Cultural Arts Center. *African Memories 2*. Minneapolis, Minn.
Aguet, Isabelle. *A Pictorial History of the Slave Trade*. Translated by Bonnie Christen. Geneva: Editions Minerva, 1971.
Ajayi, J. F. A., and Michael Crowder, eds. *History of West Africa*. Vol. 1. 2d ed. New York: Columbia University Press, 1976.
———. *History of West Africa*. Vol. 2. New York: Columbia University Press, 1973.
Aptheker, Herbert. *American Negro Slave Revolts*. New York: International Publishers, 1974.
———. *A Documentary History of the Negro People in the United States from Colonial Times to 1910*. New York: Citadel Press, 1969.
———. *Essays in the History of the American Negro*. New York: International Publishers, 1964.
Balandier, Georges, and Jacques Maquet. *Dictionary of Black African Civilization*. New York: Leon Amiel, Publishers, 1974.
Bennett, Lerone, Jr. *Pioneers in Protest*. Baltimore: Penguin Books, 1969.
Berlin, Ira. *Slaves Without Masters*. New York: Random House, Vintage Books, 1976.
Bethell, Leslie. *The Abolition of the Brazilian Slave Trade: Britain, Brazil and the Slave Trade Question, 1807-1869*. Cambridge: At the University Press, 1970.
Bibb, Henry. *Narrative of the Life and Adventures of Henry Bibb, An American Slave, Written by Himself*. 1850. Reprint. Philadelphia: Historic Publications, 1969.
Boahen, A. Adu; J. Desmond Clark; John Henrik Clarke et al. *The Horizon History of Africa*. 2 vols. American Heritage Publishing Co., Inc., 1971.
Brawley, Benjamin. *A Social History of the American Negro*. New York: Macmillan Publishing Co., Inc., Collier Books, 1970.
Brooks, Lester. *Great Civilizations of Ancient Africa*. New York: Four Winds Press, 1971.
Bruce, Kathleen. *Virginia Iron Manufacture in the Slave Era*. 1930. Reprint. New York: Augustus M. Kelly Publishers, 1968.
Bruns, Roger, ed. *Am I Not a Man and a Brother: The Antislavery Crusade of Revolutionary America, 1688-1788*. New York: Chelsea House Publishers, in association with R. R. Bowker Co., 1977.
Buell, Raymond Leslie. *Liberia: A Century of Survival, 1847-1947*. 1947. Reprint. New York: Kraus Reprint Co., 1969.
Carroll, Joseph Cephas. *Slave Insurrections in the United States 1800-1865*. New York: Negro Universities Press, 1938.

Cartey, Winfred, and Martin Kilson, eds. *The African Reader: Colonial Africa.* New York: Random House, Vintage Books, 1970.

Chambers, Bradford, ed. *Chronicles of Black Protest.* New York and Scarborough, Ontario: New American Library, Mentor Books, 1968. [Original title: *Chronicles of Negro Protest*]

Cobb, Thomas R. R. *An Inquiry into the Law of Negro Slavery . . .* 1858. Reprint. New York: Negro Universities Press, 1968.

Curtin, Philip D. *The Atlantic Slave Trade.* Madison: University of Wisconsin Press, 1969.

Dabbs, Edith M. *Face of an Island: Leigh Richmond Miner's Photographs of Saint Helena Island.* South Carolina: R. L. Bryan Co., 1970.

Davidson, Basil. *Africa in History: Themes and Outlines.* New York: Macmillan Publishing Co., Inc., 1968.

————. *African Kingdoms. Great Ages of Man. New York: Time-Life Books, 1966.*

————. *The Growth of African Civilisation: West Africa 1000-1800.* London: Longmans, Green and Co., Ltd., 1965.

————, with F. K. Buah and the advice of J. F. Ade Ajayi. *A History of West Africa to the Nineteenth Century.* Garden City, N.Y.: Doubleday & Co., Inc., Anchor Books, 1966.

DeGraft-Johnson, J. C. *African Glory: The Story of Vanished Negro Civilizations.* London: Watts and Co., 1954.

Delany, M. R., and Howard H. Bell. *Search for a Place: Black Separatism and Africa, 1860.* Ann Arbor: University of Michigan Press, 1971.

Dictionary of African Biography (The Encyclopaedia Africana). Vol. 1, *Ethiopia-Ghana.* Editor-in-Chief: L. H. Ofosu-Appiah. New York: Reference Publications, Inc., 1977.

Diggs, Irene. *Chronology of Notable Events and Dates in the History of the African and His Descendants During the Period of Slavery and the Slave Trade.* [Pamphlet] ASNLH, Inc., 1970.

Dorson, Richard M. *African Folklore.* New York: Doubleday & Co., Inc., Anchor Books, 1972.

Dow, George Francis. *Slave Ships and Slaving.* 1927. Reprint. Westport, Conn.: Negro Universities Press, 1970.

Driskell, David S., with catalog notes by Leonard Simon. *Two Centuries of Black American Art.* [Catalog] New York: Alfred A. Knopf, with the Los Angeles County Museum of Art, 1976.

Du Bois, W. E. B. *The World and Africa. . . .* New York: Viking Press, 1947.

Du Bois, W. E. Burghardt. *The Suppression of the African Slave-Trade to the United States of America, 1638-1870.* Reprint. Sourcebooks in Negro History. New York: Schocken Books, 1971.

Fage, J. D. *An Atlas of African History.* London: Edward Arnold (Publishers) Ltd., 1958.

————. *Ghana: A Historical Interpretation.* Madison: University of Wisconsin Press, 1966.

Foner, Eric, ed. *Nat Turner.* Great Lives Observed. Englewood Cliffs, N.J.: Prentice-Hall, Inc., 1971.

Foner, Laura, and Eugene D. Genovese, eds. *Slavery in the New World: A Reader in Comparative History.* Englewood Cliffs, N.J.: Prentice-Hall, Inc., 1969.

Foner, Philip S., ed. *The Voice of Black America . . .* New York: Simon and Schuster, Inc., 1972.

Franklin, John Hope. *From Slavery to Freedom.* 4th ed. New York: Alfred A. Knopf, Inc., 1974.

Garrison, William Lloyd. *Thoughts on African Colonization.* 1832. Reprint. New

York: Arno Press and *The New York Times,* 1968.

Gutman, Herbert. *The Black Family in Slavery and Freedom, 1750-1925.* New York: Pantheon Books, 1976.

Hallett, Robin. *Africa to 1875: A Modern History.* Ann Arbor: University of Michigan Press, 1970.

Harris, Middleton; Morris Levitt; Roger Furman; Ernest Smith. *The Black Book.* Edited by Toni Morrison. New York: Random House, Inc., 1974.

Harris, Sheldon H. *Paul Cuffee.* New York: Simon and Schuster, Inc., 1972.

Headley, J. T. *The Great Riots of New York, 1712 to 1873.* Miami, Fla.: Mnemosyne Publishing Co., Inc., 1969.

———. *Pen and Pencil Sketches of the Great Riots.* 1882. Reprint. Miami, Fla.: Mnemosyne Publishing Co., Inc., 1969.

Herskovits, Melville J. *The Myth of the Negro Past.* Boston: Beacon Press, 1958.

Huggins, Nathan Irvin. *Black Odyssey: The Afro-American Ordeal in Slavery.* New York: Pantheon Books, 1977.

———. Martin Kilson; and Daniel M. Fox, editors. *Key Issues in the Afro-American Experience.* New York: Harcourt Brace Jovanovich, Inc., 1971.

Hughes, Langston, and Milton Meltzer. *A Pictorial History of the Negro in America.* 3d rev. ed. New York: Crown Publishers, Inc., 1968.

Hughes, Langston, and Arna Bontemps, eds. *The Poetry of the Negro: 1746-1970.* Garden City, N.Y.: Doubleday and Co., Inc., 1970.

Ingraham, Leonard W. *Slavery in the United States.* New York: Franklin Watts, Inc., 1968.

Jackson, John G. *Introduction to African Colonization.* Introduction and additional bibliographical notes by John Henrick Clark. New York: University Books, 1971.

James, C. L. R. *The Black Jacobins: Toussaint L'Ouverture and the San Domingo Revolution.* 2d ed. New York: Random House, 1963.

———. *A History of Pan-African Revolts.* 2d ed., rev. Washington, D.C.: Drum and Spear Press, 1969.

Jay, William. *An Inquiry into the Character and Tendency of the American Colonization and American Anti-Slavery Societies.* 1835. Reprint. New York: Kraus Reprint Co., 1969.

Jefferson, Thomas. *Thomas Jefferson's Farm Book. . . .* Edited by Edwin Morris Betts. Charlottesville: University Press of Virginia, 1976.

Kaplan, Sidney. *The Black Presence in the Era of the American Revolution, 1770-1800.* Greenwich, Conn.: New York Graphic Society, in association with the Smithsonian Institution Press, 1973.

Klemp, Egon. *Africa on Maps Dating from the Twelfth to the Eighteenth Century. . . .* New York: Holmes & Meier Publishers, Inc., 1972.

Korngold, Ralph. *Citizen Toussaint.* New York: Hill and Wang, 1965.

The Library Company of Philadelphia. *Negro History: 1553-1903. . . .* [Catalog] Philadelphia, 1969.

Lofton, John. *Insurrection in South Carolina: The Turbulent World of Denmark Vesey.* Yellow Springs, Ohio: Antioch Press, 1964.

Logan, Rayford W., and Irving S. Cohen. *The American Negro: Old World Background and New World Experience.* Rev. ed., edited by Howard R. Anderson. Boston: Houghton Mifflin Co., 1970.

Lynch, Hollis R. *Edward Wilmot Blyden: Pan-Negro Patriot, 1832-1912.* New York: Oxford University Press, 1967.

Mannix, Daniel R., in collaboration with Malcolm Cowley. *Black Cargoes: A History of the Atlantic Slave Trade, 1518-1865.* New York: Viking Press, 1962.

Maugham, R. C. F. *The Republic of Liberia.* 1920. Reprint. New York: Negro Universities Press, 1969.

Meauzé, Pierre. *African Art: Sculpture.* Cleveland and New York: World Publishing Co., 1968.

Morison, Samuel Eliot. *Admiral of the Ocean Sea.* Boston: Little, Brown & Co., 1942.

Mphahlele, Ezekiel. *The African Image.* Rev. ed. New York: Praeger Publishers, 1974.

Murphy, E. Jefferson. *History of African Civilization.* New York: Dell Publishing Co., Inc., 1972.

Museum of African Art. *African Art in Washington Collections.* [Catalog] Washington, D.C., 1972.

————. *The Language of African Art.* [Catalog] Washington, D.C., 1970.

Nevinson, Henry W. *A Modern Slavery.* 1906. Reprint. New York: Schocken Books, 1968.

Ofari, Earl. *"Let Your Motto Be Resistance": The Life and Thought of Henry Highland Garnet.* Boston: Beacon Press, 1972.

Ofosu-Appiah, L. H. *People in Bondage: African Slavery in the Modern Era.* Minneapolis, Minn.: Lerner Publications Co., 1971.

————. *Slavery: A Brief Survey.* Accra, Ghana: Waterville Publishing House, 1969.

Oliver, Roland, and Anthony Atmore. *Africa Since 1800.* 2d ed. Cambridge: Cambridge University Press, 1972.

Owen, Nicholas. *Nicholas Owen Journal of a Slave Dealer . . . 1746-1757.* Edited by Evaline Marton. London, 1930.

Owen, Robert. *The Wrong of Slavery: The Right of Emancipation . . .* 1864. Reprint. New York: Kraus Reprint Co., 1969.

Parrinder, Geoffrey. *African Mythology.* London: Hamlyn Publishing Group, Ltd., 1967.

Perham, Margery, and J. Simmons, eds. *African Discovery: An Anthology of Exploration.* Evanston, Ill.: Northwestern University Press, 1963.

Philadelphia Museum of Art. *Impact Africa: African Art and the West.* [Catalog] Inaugural Exhibition of the Bernice McIlhenny Wintersteen Student Center, January 24-June 30, 1969.

Phillips, Wendell. *Speeches, Lectures, and Letters.* 2d series. Boston: Lee and Shepard, 1905.

Ploski, Harry A., and Warren Marr II, eds. *The Negro Almanac: A Reference Work on the Afro American.* Bicentennial ed. New York: Bellwether Co., 1976.

Porter, Dale, H. *The Abolition of the Slave Trade in England, 1784-1807.* Hamden, Conn.: Archon Books, 1970.

Quarles, Benjamin. *Black Abolitionists.* New York: Oxford University Press, 1969.

————. *The Negro in the American Revolution.* New York: W. W. Norton & Co., Inc., 1973.

Ransford, Oliver. *The Slave Trade: The Story of Transatlantic Slavery.* London: John Murray, 1971.

Redkey, Edwin S. *Black Exodus.* Yale Publications in American Studies No. 17. New Haven and London: Yale University Press, 1969.

Robinson, Ronald; John Gallagher; and Alice Denny. *Africa and the Victorians: The Climax of Imperialism.* Garden City, N.Y.: Doubleday & Co., Inc., Anchor Books, 1968.

Rodney, Walter. *West Africa and the Atlantic Slave-Trade.* Reprint 6. Africa Research Group. Chicago: New World Research Center, n.d.

Rogers, J. A. *World's Great Men of Color.* Vol. II. New York: Collier Books, 1972.

Rollin, Frank A. *Life and Public Services of Martin R. Delany . . .* 1883. Reprint. New York: Arno Press and The New York Times, 1969.

Rotberg, Robert I. *A Political History of Tropical Africa.* New York: Harcourt Brace & World, Inc., 1965.

Sadler, Michael E., ed. *Arts of West Africa (Excluding Music).* London: Oxford University Press, 1935.

Salk, Erwin A. *A Layman's Guide to Negro History.* New York: McGraw-Hill Book Co., A Ramparts Book, 1967.

Shinnie, Margaret. *Ancient African Kingdoms.* New York: New American Library, Mentor Books, 1965.

Simmons, William J. *Men of Mark.* 1887. Reprint. Ebony Classics. Chicago: Johnson Publishing Co., Inc., 1970.

Snowden, Frank M., Jr. *Blacks in Antiquity: Ethiopians in the Greco-Roman Experience.* Cambridge: Belknap Press at Harvard University Press, 1970.

Sweeney, James Johnson. *African Negro Art.* New York: Museum of Modern Art, 1935.

Thompson, Robert Farris. *African Art in Motion: Icon and Act in the Collection of Katherine Coryton White.* Berkeley and Los Angeles: University of California Press, 1974.

Tragle, Henry Irving, ed. *The Southampton Slave Revolt of 1831: A Compilation of Source Material.* Amherst: University of Massachusetts Press, 1971.

Vlahos, Olivia. *African Beginnings.* New York: Viking Press, 1967.

Ward, W. E. F. *The Royal Navy and the Slavers: The Suppression of the Atlantic Slave Trade.* New York: Random House, Pantheon Books, 1969.

Washington, George. *The Writings of George Washington, 1745-1799.* Edited by John C. Fitzpatrick. Washington, D.C.: U.S. Government Printing Office, 1931-44.

Williams, Chancellor. *The Destruction of Black Civilization: Great Issues of a Race from 4500 B.C. to 2000 A.D.* Chicago: Third World Press, 1974.

Williams, Eric. *Capitalism and Slavery.* New York: G. P. Putnam's Sons, 1966.

Wilson, Charles Morrow. *Liberia: Black Africa in Microcosm.* New York: Harper & Row Pubs., Inc., 1971.

Wood, Peter H. *Black Majority.* New York: W. W. Norton & Co., Inc., 1974.

Articles and Periodicals

Bauer, Raymond A., and Alice H. Bauer. "Day to Day Resistance to Slavery." *The Journal of Negro History.* 27 (1942): 388-419.

Bell, Howard H. "Negro Nationalism: A Factor in Emigration Projects, 1858-1861." *The Journal of Negro History* 47 (1962): 42-53.

Blackett, Richard. "Martin R. Delany and Robert Campbell: Black Americans in Search of an African Colony." *The Journal of Negro History* 62 (1977): 1-25.

Boyd, Willis D. "The American Colonization Society and the Slave Recaptives of 1860-1861: An Early Example of United States-African Relations." *The Journal of Negro History* 47 (1962): 108-126.

Brewer, W. M. "Henry Highland Garnet." *The Journal of Negro History* 13 (1928): 36-52.

Brewer, William M. "John B. Russwurm." *The Journal of Negro History* 13 (1928): 413-422.

Brown, Kenneth I. "Color and Christian Missions in Africa." *The Journal of Religious Thought* 23 (1966-67): 51-59.

Cadbury, Henry J. "Negro Membership in the Society of Friends." *The Journal of Negro History* 21 (1936): 151-213.

Carlson, Fred A. "Negro Culture in Two Continents—A General Discussion." *The*

Journal of Negro History 27 (1942): 68-70.

Cleven, N. Andrew N. "Some Plans of Colonizing Liberated Negro Slaves in Hispanic America." *The Journal of Negro History* 11 (1926): 35-49.

Cromwell, John W. "The Aftermath of Nat Turner's Insurrection." *The Journal of Negro History* 5 (1920): 208-234.

David, C. W. A. "The Fugitive Slave Law of 1793 and its Antecedents." *The Journal of Negro History* 9 (1924): 18-25.

Davies, Everetts F. S. "The Negro Protest Movement: The Religious Way." *The Journal of Religious Thought* 24 (1967-68): 13-35.

Dillard, Irving, "James Milton Turner: A Little Known Benefactor of His People." *The Journal of Negro History* 19 (1934): 372-411.

Dowd, Jerome. "Slavery and the Slave Trade in Africa." *The Journal of Negro History* 2 (1917): 1-20.

Fisher, Miles Mark. "Lott Cary, The Colonizing Missionary." *The Journal of Negro History* 7 (1922): 380-418.

Foster, Charles I. "The Colonization of Free Negroes, in Liberia, 1816-1835." *The Journal of Negro History* 38 (1953): 41-66.

Gordon, A. H. "The Struggle of the Negro Slaves for Physical Freedom." *The Journal of Negro History* 13 (1928): 22-35.

Greene, Lorenzo J. "Mutiny on the Slave Ships." *Phylon* 5 (1944): 346-354.

Harris, Sheldon H. "An American's Impression of Sierra Leone in 1811." *The Journal of Negro History* 47 (1962): 35-41.

Johnston, James Hugo. "The Participation of White Men in Virginia Negro Insurrections." *The Journal of Negro History* 16 (1931): 158-167.

Kates, Don B., Jr. "Abolition, Deportation, Integration: Attitudes Toward Slavery in the Early Republic." *The Journal of Negro History* 53 (1968): 33-47.

Landon, Fred. "Henry Bibb, A Colonizer." *The Journal of Negro History* 5 (1920): 437-447.

————. "The Negro Migration to Canada After the Passing of the Fugitive Slave Act." *The Journal of Negro History* 5 (1920): 22-36.

Laughon, Samuel W. "Administrative Problems in Maryland in Liberia—1836-1851." *The Journal of Negro History* 26: 325-364.

McDougle, Ivan E. "Public Opinion Regarding Emancipation and Colonization." *The Journal of Negro History* 3 (1918): 303-328.

McLaughlin, Tom L. "Sectional Responses of Free Negroes to the Idea of Colonization." *Research Studies* 34 (1966): 123-134.

Mehlinger, Louis R. "The Attitude of the Free Negro Toward African Colonization." *The Journal of Negro History* 1 (1916): 376-301.

Miles, Edwin A. "The Mississippi Slave Insurrection Scare of 1835." *The Journal of Negro History* 42 (1957): 48-60.

Morsell, John A. "Black Nationalism." *The Journal of Intergroup Relations* 8 (Winter 1961-62): 5-11.

Mower, J. H. "The Republic of Liberia." *The Journal of Negro History* 32 (1947): 265-305.

Patton, James W. "The Progress of Emancipation in Tennessee, 1796-1860." *The Journal of Negro History* 17 (1932): 67-102.

Redkey, Edwin S. "Bishop Turner's African Dream." *The Journal of American History* 54 (1967): 271-290.

Rippy, J. Fred. "A Negro Colonization Project in Mexico, 1895." *The Journal of Negro History* 6 (1921): 66-73.

Scott, Kenneth. "The Slave Insurrection in New York in 1712." *The New-York Historical Society Quarterly,* 45 (1961): 43-74.

Seifman, Eli. "Education or Emigration: The Schism Within the African Colonization Movement, 1865-1906." *History of Education Quarterly* 7 (Spring 1967): 36-57.

Sherwood, Henry Noble. "Paul Cuffe." *The Journal of Negro History* 8 (1923): 153-232.

Szasz, Ferenc M. "The New-York Slave Revolt of 1741: A Re-Examination." *New York History* 48 (1967): 215-230.

Scheips, Paul J. "Lincoln and the Chiriqui Colonization Project." *The Journal of Negro History* 37 (1952): 418-453.

Wax, Darold D. "Negro Resistance to the Early American Slave Trade." *The Journal of Negro History* 51 (1966): 1-15.

———. "A Philadelphia Surgeon on a Slaving Voyage to Africa, 1749-1751." *The Pennsylvania Magazine of History and Biography* 92 (1968): 465-493.

Weisbord, Robert G. "The Back-to-Africa Idea." *History Today* 18 (1968): 30-37.

Wesley, Charles H. "Lincoln's Plan for Colonizing the Emancipated Negroes." *The Journal of Negro History* (1919): 7-21.

Wilson, Nan. "Legal Attitudes to Slavery in Eighteenth-Century Britain; English Myth; Scottish Social Realism and Their Wider Comparative Context." *Race: The Journal of the Institute of Race Relations* 11. 4 (1970): 463-475.

Wish, Harvey. "American Slave Insurrections Before 1861." *The Journal of Negro History* 22 (1937): 299-320.

INDEX

Page numbers in italics refer to illustrations.

A

Abolitionist movement, 57–58, 61, *160–173*
Abu Bakr. *See* Ibn-Umar
Adams, John, 52
Adams, John Quincy, 65; 109, *136, 169;* let-
  ter from, *138*
Adanse, 33
"An Address to the Slaves of the United
  States" (Garnet), 184
Adrar, 21
Adventure (ship), *92*
African Institute in New York, 77
African Methodist Episcopal Church, 58,
  67
African Methodist Episcopal Zion Church,
  77
African Presbyterian Church, 170
*African Repository and Colonial Journal,
  The,* 63
Africanus, Leo: 29; quoted, 27; 27 (*n.*)
Agassiz, Louis, 111
Agriculture: discovery of in Africa, 19
Akan (people), 32–34
Allegheny Mountains, 55
Allen, Elizabeth, 108
Allen, Richard, 57, *58,* 67, 180, 182
Alligator (ship), *186*
Almoravids, 21, 22, 33, 34
American Anti-Slavery Society, 143
American Colonization Society: 61–64, 67,
  177, 179, 183, 186, 188, 189, 190, 195; let-
  ter to, *65*
American Missionary Association, 139
"American Society for Colonizing the Free
  People of Colour of the United States,
  The." *See* American Colonization Soci-
  ety
Annapolis Royal, Nova Scotia, Canada,
  59–60
Antislavery movement, 57, 61
Aoukar. *See* Ghana (Ancient)
Arab: scholars, 23, 27; traders in Africa,
  22, 23
Asante (people), 33
Ashanti (people): 29, *72,* 84; goldweights
  of, *84*
Ashmun, Jehudi: 64, 66, *66;* quoted, 64, 65
Ashmun Street (Monrovia, Liberia), *194*

Asiento, 41
"Askia the Great." *See* Askia Muhammad
Askia Muhammad: 24, 25, 26, 27; tomb of,
  26, *28*
Askia Musa, 26
As-Sadi, 24
Assyria, 19
Atlantic Ocean, 19, 23, 35
Augusta (ship), 65
Autobiography of a Fugitive Negro
  (Ward), 168
Awdaghast (Audoghast), 22
Axim. *See* Slave forts
Azores, 37

B

Badger, George E., 154
Baldwin, Roger Sherman: 136; letter to,
  138
Baltimore (Md.), 67
Banneker, Benjamin: quoted, 44
Barbados: and the slave trade, 45, 92
Baule (people), 85
Beecher, Henry Ward, *169*
Bell, Phillip A., *183*
Bello, Ahmadu, 30
Benezet, Anthony, 57, 167
Benin, 87
Bennett, Bryant, 120
Bennett, Elizabeth, 120
Bennett, Gov. Thomas, 131
Berbers (people), 21, 32
Bight of Benin, 42
Black codes, 53, 107
Blyden, Edward Wilmot, *68*
Bonaparte, Napoleon, 48, 50, 53
Bornu, 30, 31, 42
Bouré, 23
Bowser, David Bustill, 144
Brawley, Benjamin: quoted, 63
Brazil, 41
Breda. *See* L'Ouverture, Toussaint
Brookes (ship), *91*
Brown, John: 52, 130, 143, *144,* 144, 166;
  raid of, 55, *144–148*

Brown, Moses, *166, 167*
Brown, William Wells, *168*
Brutus, Marcus Junius, 52 (*n.*)
Bryant, William Cullen, *169*
Bulala (people), 32
Burns, Anthony, 171
Bushrod's Island (Liberia), 64, 190
Buxton, Thomas: letter from, *164*

C

Caerlof, Henry, 41, 42
Cameroon, 30, 32, 44
Campbell, William, 134
Cantine, John, 149
Cape Coast Castle. *See* Slave forts
Cape of Good Hope, 37, 80
Cape Mesurado (Liberia), 64, 65, 66, *188, 189. See also* Monrovia
Cape Palmas (Liberia), 69, *199*
Cap-Haïtien (Hispaniola), 38
Caravans: in Africa, 27, 37, *82*; map of, *26*
Caravel, 37, *38*
Caribbean: colonization in, 61; exploration of, 38, 40; plantations of, 38, 42; slave revolts in, 47–52; slavery in, 38, 40, 45, 46, 62
Cary, Lott, 66
Catawbaw (people), 130
Catholic Church: and slavery, 40–41
Cavalla River. *See* Rivers
Chad, 31, 32
Charleston, S.C.: and the slave trade, 45, 77, 92, 108, 127, 128
Charleston, Va. (now W. Va.), 145
Charlson (?), George H., 55
Chicasaws (people), 130
Chi Wara headdress, *87*
Christiansborg. *See* Slave forts
Cinqué Joseph: *136;* mutiny led by, *136–140, 139*
Clarkson, Thomas: 57, 60, *163;* letter to, *164;* quoted, 57; 47 (*n.*)
Clay, Cassius M., *169*
Clay, Henry: 62-63; quoted, 63
Clinton, Sir Henry, 59
Coker, Rev. Daniel, *67*
Colonization movement: 57, 59-61, *174-179;* resistance to, *180–185*
Colson, William: memorandum book of, *192;* passport of, *191*
Columbus, Christopher: 35, 37, *37*, 38, 40; quoted, 39
Columbus, Diego, 38, 40
Comtoste, C.: letter from, *148*
The Condition, Elevation, Emigration, and Destiny of the Colored People of the United States Politically Considered (Delany), 185
Congress (U.S.), 44, 54, 58, 62, 64, 178
Considerations on Keeping Negroes . . .

(Woolman), 57 (*n.*)
Constitution of the Liberian Republic, 69
Continental Army (American), 58
Continental Congress, 52
Cornish, Samuel, *167*
Cotton: 62; and slavery, 54
Cromwell, Oliver, 50
Crummell, Alexander, *198*
Cuffe, Paul: *62,* 77, *177;* compass of, *63;* letters from, *176, 177*

D

Dan Fodio, Osman, 30
Danish West Indies, 68
Daphne (ship), 186
"Dark-continent" myth, 19
Deas, David, 108
Deas, John, 108
Declaration of Independence: (American) 44; (Liberian) 69
DeGraft-Johnson, J. C., 34
Delany, Maj. Martin R., 68, 184, *185*
De las Casas, Bartolomé, 40
Dembia River. *See* Rivers
De'Medici, Giovanni Leo. *See* Africanus, Leo
Denmark: and the slave trade, 42
De Ovando, Nicolas, 40
Dixcove. *See* Slave forts
Documents from the Navy Department Accompanying the President's Message, 64, 66 (*n.*)
Dogon (people), 72
Douglass, Frederick: 143, 152, 168, *185;* quoted, 44, 143
Dubois, Felix: quoted, 27
Du Bois, W. E. B.: quoted, 35, 45, 46, 200
Dun-lore, 144
Dutch. *See* Netherlands
Dutch West India Company, 41, 52

E

Egungun Society: 73; mask of, *73*
Egypt: 19, 32; and Mali, 23
Elford, W.: letter to, *165*
Elk-Hill, 114
Ellis, Anderson, 125
Ellis, John W., 125
Elmina Castle. *See* Slave forts
Emerson, Rev. Ralph Waldo, 197
England: and abolition of slavery, 54, 57, 59, 60, 61, *160, 163–165;* and colonization, 59-61, 66; and the Caribbean, 47, 49; and the Protestant Reformation, 39; and the slave trade, 41, 100, 101
Ennals, Samuel, 183
Epa Society: 88; mask of, *88*
Era of the Common Man, 54

Ethiopia, 35
Ethno-history, 27-28
Exeter Hall, *163*

F

Fante: language, 33; people, 33
Fayette. *See* LaFayette
Feudalism, 46
Finley, Robert: letter to, *177*
Fort Amsterdam. *See* Slave forts
Fort Carolusburg (Cape Coast Castle). *See* Slave forts
Forten, James: 180, 181; letter to, *176*
Foster, Dwight, 166
Foura Bay (Liberia), 67
France: and the Caribbean, 47-50, 61; and the slave trade, 41, 42, 101
Franklin, Benjamin: 57, 58, 77; letter from, *161; 57 (n.)*
Free African Society, 58, 182
Freedom's Journal (newspaper), 167, 195
Freetown (Sierra Leone), 61
Frobenius, Leo: quoted, 19
Fugitive Slave Law, 141-143, 152
Fulani (people), 30, 32
Futa Toro (people), 25

G

Gambia River. *See* Rivers
Gao (Mali), 23, 26
Garnet, Henry Highland, 56, 68, *184*
Garrison, William Lloyd, 167, 168, *169*, *176*
Gelede Society: 89; mask of, *73, 89*
Georgia: and slavery, 53
Ghana: (Ancient) 20-22; 23, 33, 34; map of, *21;* (modern), 29, 33, 34, 84
Giddings, Joshua R., *169*
Gloucester, John, *170*
Gobir, 30
Gold Coast, 33, 34, 42, 100. *See also* Ghana
Gold trade: in West Africa, 21, 22, 23, 24, 29
Gordon, Rev. N. M.: letter to *179*
Grain Coast, 44
Grand Bassa (Liberia), 68
Grant, Ulyssess S., 155
Great Britain. *See* England
Greece: and slavery, 40
Greenhill's Point (Cape Coast Castle). *See* Slave forts
Greenville (Liberia), 69
Guan: language, 33; people, 33
Guinea, 20, 35
Guinea Coast, 42
Gulf of Benin, 19
Gulf of Guinea, 35, 41
Gulf of Mexico, 53
Gurley, Rev. R. R., 67

H

Haiti: 38, 53, 61, 101; revolution in, 47-50, 170
Hall, Prince, 53
Hallett, Robin: quoted, 19
Hampden, John, 52 (*n.*)
Harper, Robert Goodloe, 69 (*n.*)
Harper's Ferry, 144-146, 148
Hausa: people, 32, *83;* States, 26, 28, 29-31; map of, *30*
Haydon, Benjamin R.: painting by, *163*
Henry, Joseph, 198
Henry the Navigator, Prince of Portugal, 35, *74*
Henry, Patrick: quoted, 44
Hispaniola, 38, 39. *See also* Haiti
Holy Roman Empire, 39
House of Commons (British), 43
House of Representatives, 62-63, 109, 184
Howland, Thomas, *78*
Hubard, R. T.: slave journal of, *121*
Hughes, Langston: 2 ("The Negro Speaks of Rivers"); 202 ("A Ballad of Negro History," attributed to)
Human Rights (newspaper), *173*

I

Ibn-Batutu, 29
Ibn Hawqal, 21
Ibn Muhammad al-Wazzan as-Zayyate. *See* Africanus, Leo
Ibn-Umar, Abu, Bakr, 22, 33
Ibn-Yasin, Abdallah, 21
Ibo (people), 88
Inbn-Ibrahim, Yahya, 21
Indian Ocean, 35
Indians (Native Americans): and slavery, 38-40
Industrial Revolution, 45, 46, 61
Iron Age: in Africa, 19, 20
Isabella, Queen of Castile and Aragon, 39
Islam: and Ancient Ghana, 21, 22; and Berbers, 21, 31; and feudalism, 46; and Hausa States, 28, 30, 31; and Kanem-Bornu, 28, 32; and Mali, 23; and Modern Ghana, 34; and Mossi States, 28; and Portuguese, 35; and Songhai, 24, 25, 26; and trans-Saharan trade, 20
Ivory Coast, 44, 85, 86, 89, 90

J

Jamaica: 48-49; and slavery, *102-105,* 108
James, C. L. R.: quoted, 48
Jarvis, John Wesley, 166
Jefferson, Thomas: 48, 53, 54; quoted, 44, 61; records kept by, *113–118*

Jocelyn, Nathaniel, 136
John II, King of Portugal, 35
Johnson, Elijah, 66
John Street Methodist Episcopal Church, 77
Jones, Absalom: 57, 58, 180, *182;* sermon by, *182*
Journal . . . of Donations for Education in Liberia, 197

K

Kanem, 28, 31, 33, 34
Kanem-Bornu: 28, 31-32; map of, *31;* European division of, 32. *See also* Bornu and Kanem
Kanembu (dynasty), 32
Kangaba (state), 24
Kano (city-state), 30, 32
Kanuri (people), 32
Katsina (city-state), 30
Kente cloth, *72*
Key, Francis Scott, *65*
Kidnapped and Ransomed, The (Still), 156
Kinney, Henry E.: painting attributed to, *166*
Kong Mountains, 19
Kormantine. *See* Slave forts
Kotoko (people), 32
Kru Bay (Sierra Leone), 61

L

La Amistad (ship): *136;* mutiny on, *136–140,* 146
LaFayette, Marquis de, 52 (*n.*)
Lake Chad, 31, 32, 34
Latrobe, John H.: painting by, *195*
Laws of the Indies (1542), 39
Lear, Tobias: 61; letter to, *51;* quoted, 59
Lee, William, 59
L'Eliza (ship), 186
Lennox & Deas, 108
Lexington, Ken.: and slave resistance, 55
Liberia: 186; colonization of, 64-69, 78, *186–199;* motto of, 69, *69*
Liberia College, 198
Liberia Herald (newspaper), 195
Libya, 32
Lincoln, Abraham, 61
Linn, Joseph A., 125
Livingstone, David, 19
London World Antislavery Conference, *163*
Louisiana: and slave resistance, 55
Louisiana Territory: and slavery, 52, 53; purchase of, 48, 53
L'Ouverture, Toussaint: 47-52, *49,* 61; letter from, *51;* quoted, 48

Lovejoy, Owen, *169*
Lundy, Benjamin, *169*
Luther, Martin, 39

M

Macandel, 47 (*n.*). *See also* Maroons
MacNeilly, Robert: letter from, *179*
Madeira, 35
Madison, James, *179*
Mahmoud Kati, 28
Mali: (ancient) 20, 22-24, 26, 27; map of, *22;* (modern) 20, *72*
Malinke (people), 23
Mandara (people), 32
Mandingo (people), 23, 28
Mankessim (city), 33
Manoralism, 46
Mansa Kankan Musa. *See* Mansa Musa
Mansa Musa: *22, 23, 24, 27, 75;* mosque of, 26; pilgrimage to Mecca, 23
Maroons: 46, 47; chiefs (Père Jean, Michel, Colas, Polydor, Macandel, Canga, Santiague, Jean-François, Biassou), 47
Martinique: and slavery, 47
Mary Caroline Stevens (ship), *96*
Maryland Colony (Liberia), 69, *195, 195*
Mason-Dixon Line, 143
Massachusetts: and slave resistance, 53
Mathilde (ship), 186
Mauritania, 20, 21
Mecca, 21, 23, 25
Mediterranean Sea, 20, 27
"Memorial Discourse" (Garnet), *184*
Mende (people), 85, 136
Mesopotamia: and slavery, 40
Midas (ship), *172*
Middle passage, 42, 43, 96
Mikell, Edward, W., 128
Mississippi in Africa (Liberia), 69
Mississippi River, 53
Mmwo Society: 88; mask of, *88*
Mole St. Nicholas (Haiti), 48
Monkey (ship), *172*
Monroe, James, 69 (*n.*)
Monrovia (Liberia), 69, 69 (*n.*), 187, *188, 190,* 192, *194*
Monticello, 113, 114
Morocco: and Mali, 23; and Songhai, 26; and Timbuktu, 27
Mossi: people, 25; states, 23, 28-29; map of, *29*
Mother Bethel African Methodist Episcopal Church, *180*
"Mother-right," 33
Mount Olivet Baptist Church, *186*
Mount Vernon, 59, 62, 64
Mountains of the Moon, 80
Muhammad Turé. *See* Askia Muhammad
Muslim-Berbers, 21
Mythology (African), 24

N

Negro Convention Movement, 68, 183, 184
Netherlands: and slave trade, 41, 100, 101
New Bedford, Mass., 62
New Brunswick (Canada), 60
New Orleans, La.: and black codes, 53
Newport, R.I.: and slave trade, 92
Newton, A.P., 19
New York: and slave resistance, 53, 106; and slavery, 52, *106*
New York State Colonization Society, 68, 69
Niger Delta, 44
Nigeria, 30, 32, 73, 76, 87, 88, 89, 90
Niger River. *See* Rivers
Nile River. *See* Rivers
Noisette, Philip Stanislas, 151
Notes on Virginia (Jefferson), 44
Nova Scotia (Canada), 59-60, 61
Nubia, 20
Nupe (Nigeria), *76*

O

Oburumankuma, 33
O'Connel, Daniel, *163*
Odapagyan, 33
Odudua (mythological being), 89
Ogé, Vincent, 47 (*n.*)
"On Mixed Races in Liberia" (Blyden), 68
Osom, 33
Ouagadougou (kingdom), 29
Oya (mythological being), 90

P

Pahbah, 32
Palmer and Ackerman Salt Manufacturing Company, 148; letter to, *147*
Pan-Africanism, 68
Parker, Rev. Theodore, 143
Parliament (British), 53, 59, 60, 164
Patterson, Henry J., 154
Peale, Charles Wilson, 59
Pennsylvania Colonization Society, 69
Pennsylvania Society for Promoting the Abolition of Slavery and the Relief of Free Negroes Unlawfully Held in Bondage, 58
Peru, 39
Petersburg, Va., 69, 122, 193
Peters, Thomas, 59, 61
Philadelphia Free African Society, 53
Philadelphia, Pa., 57, 67
Phillips, Wendell: *169;* quoted 50, 52
Phocion, 52 (*n.*)
Polly, Peyton: documents about, *152, 153*
Portugal: and Gold Coast, 33; and Mali, 23; and slavery, 41, 98; and Songhai, 26; and the Mandingo, 23, 24; explorations by, 35-40
Prester John, King of Abyssinia, 35, *36*
Prosser, Gabriel. *See* Slave revolts
Providence, R.I.: and the slave trade, 45, 78
Puerto Rico, 39
Purvis, Robert, *183*

Q

Quakers: and antislavery efforts, 57
Quarles, Benjamin: quoted, 58

R

Raynal, Abbé: quoted, 48
Reason, Charles, *170*
Red Sea, 27
Reformation (Protestant), 39
Regiment of Guides and Pioneers, 59
Regulation Act of 1788, 91
Redmond, Charles L., 163
Report of the Secretary of the Navy to the President of the United States, 64, 65 (*n.*)
Revolutionary War (American), 44, 47, 54, 57, 59, 166, 171, 176
Rhode Island Abolition Society, 166
Rights of All, The (newspaper), 195
Rivers (African): Cavalla, 69; Gambia, 19, 101; Niger, 19, 21, 27, 28; Nile, 19; St. John's, 68; Senegal, 19, 21, 23, 41, 47, 101; Sino, 69; Volta, 19; importance of, 19
Roberts, Colson, and Co., 192
Roberts, Jane, *193,* 194
Roberts, Joseph Jenkins, 69, 192, *193,* 193, 194
Rochambeau, Jean-Baptiste, 50 (*n.*)
Rocky Mountains, 53
Royal African Company, 94
Russwurm, John Brown: 167, *195;* letter from, *196*

S

Sahara Desert, 20, 25, *26,* 27, 31, 33
St. Helena Island (S.C.), *201-205*
St. James Island. *See* Slave forts
St. John's River. *See* Rivers
St. Louis (Africa), 41, 47
St. Thomas (Virgin Islands), 68
Santo Domingo: 39, 61; and slavery, 47; slave revolt in, 48-49
São Jorge Castle (Elmina Castle). *See* Slave forts
Sarakole (people), 28
Sartain (John): engraving by, *136*

Scott, Dred, 141, 143
Sekondi. *See* Slave forts
Senegal, 21, 23, 26
Senegal River. *See* Rivers
Senegambia, 44
Senufo (people), 33, 89, 90
Serfdom, 46
Shango (mythical being): 90; staff of, *90*
Sharp, Granville, 59, 60, *60;* letter from, *165*
Sherbro Island, 67
Shore, John K., 122
Shuwa Arabs, 32
Sidjulmassa (Sijilmasa), 22
Sierra Leone, 44, 60, 61, 62, 85, 136, 139, 177
Sierra Leone Company, 60
Sino River. *See* Rivers
Slave Coast, 42, 44
Slave codes. *See* Black codes
Slave forts: 39, 42, *98-101;* at Greenhill's Point, 100; at St. James Island, 101; Axim, 41; Cape Coast Castle, 41, *99, 100;* Christiansborg, 41; Dixcove, 41; Elmina Castle (São Jorge Castle), 35, *36,* 41, *98;* Fort Amsterdam, *100;* Fort Carolusburg, *100;* Kormantine, 41, *100;* Sekondi, 41
Slave revolts: in the Caribbean, 46-52; in Stono, S.C., 53, *130;* in the United States, 52-56; led by Denmark Vesey, 52, 55, *131;* led by Gabriel Prosser, 52, 53, 54; led by Nat Turner, 52, 55-56, *56, 132-135*
Slave trade: 43, 65, *91-101;* abolition of, 45, 59, 60; among the Europeans, 42; in the Americas, 38, 40, 41, 52, 61, 64, 68
Slavery: ancient, 40; and the Louisiana Purchase, 54; documents of, *107, 108, 109, 110, 113-129, 149-159;* in Africa, 40; in North America, 44, 46, 54, 96, *106-129;* in the Caribbean, 46, 96, *102-105;* resistance to, 52-56, 96, 106, *130-148*
Smith, Gerrit, *146, 169*
Smith, John 150
Smithsonian Institution's Annual Report (1870), 68
Society for the Abolition of the Slave Trade, 60
Sokoto: empire of, 30
Songhai, 20, 24-26, 27, 29, 30; map of, *25;* peoples, 28
Song of the Bornu Slaves, 42
Sorko (people), 24
South Carolina: and slave resistance, 53, 54
Southampton, Va.: and Nat Turner's Revolt, 55, 132, 134
Southard, Samuel L.: quoted, 65-66
Spain: and slave trade, 41; explorations by, 35-40; in the Caribbean, 47, 48, 49
Speeches, Lectures and Letters (Phillips), 50
Stanley, Henry: 19; quoted, 35
Star-Spangled Banner, The, 65
Still, Charity (Sidney), 156, *157,* 158

Still Family Memo Book, 158
Still, Levin, 156, 158; Jr., 156
Still, Peter, 156, *156,* 157, 158   159
Still, Sidney. *See* Still, Charity
Still, William, 156, 157, *157*
Stone Age: in Africa, 20
Stono River, 130
Stono, S.C. *See* Slave revolts
Sugar: and slavery, 45, 47, 54
Sully, Thomas Wilcocks: painting by, *193*
Sumner, Charles, *169*
Sundiata, 23
Sunni Ali, 24
Sunni Baru, 24, 25
Sweden: and the slave trade, 41, 42

T

Taney, Roger, 143
Tappan, Lewis, 139
Tarikh el Fettach (Mahmoud Kati), 28
Taylor, B. F., 111
Taylor, John, 119
Techiman (Ghana), 33
Teda of Tebesti, 31
Tenkodogo (city-state), 29
Thornton, William: 62; plan by, *188*
Tibesti Mountains, 31
Timbuktu, 23, 26-28, 80, *83*
Tobacco: and slavery, 47
Toussaint, François-Dominque. *See* L'Ouverture, Toussaint
Townsend, James B.: petition of, *178*
Townsend, William H.: drawings by, *139*
Trans-Saharan trade: 20, 33; and slavery, 42
Traveller (ship), 175
Triangular trade, 43, 45. *See also* Middle passage
Tuaregs (people), 23, 27, *76*
Tukular Empire, 27
Tunisia, 32
Turner, Nat. *See* Slave revolts
Twi: language, 33; people, 33

U

Underground Railroad, 157, 168, 170
Undine (ship), *173*
United States Constitution, 182

V

Vai (people), *190*
Vanderpoel, Mr.: speech of, *109*
Vesey, Denmark. *See* Slave revolts
Vesey, Sandy, 131
Vigilance Committee of Boston, 143

Virginia: and slavery, 52, 53
Virginia Provincial Convention, 44
Volta River. *See* Rivers

W

Wadai (sultanate), 31, 32
Walata (Mali), 23
Walker, David, 53, 55
Walker's Appeal, 53, 55 (*n.*)
Ward, Samuel Ringgold, *168*
Warner, Daniel Dashiel, *199*
War of 1812, 52, 176
Washington (ship), *136*
Washington, Bushrod, 62, *64,* 192
Washington, D.C., 172-173
Washington, George: 64, 190; quoted, 59
Wedgwood Josiah: 60, 77, *160,* 162; letter
   to, *161;* medallion by, *160*
Wesley, John; quoted, 41
Western Sudan, 24, 25, 33
West Indies. *See* Caribbean

Wheatley, Phillis, 58
Whitehead, Coby, 55
Whittier, John Greenleaf: 42, *169;* quoted,
   136
Wilberforce, William, 60
William, Peter, *77*
Williams, Silas, 107
Winn, Samuel, 150
Wood, Reuben, 152
Woolman, John, 57, 57 (*n.*)

Y

Yatenga (kingdom), 25, 29
Yoruba (people), 33, *73,* 88, 89, 90

Z

Zaria (city-state), 30
Zealy, J. T., 111

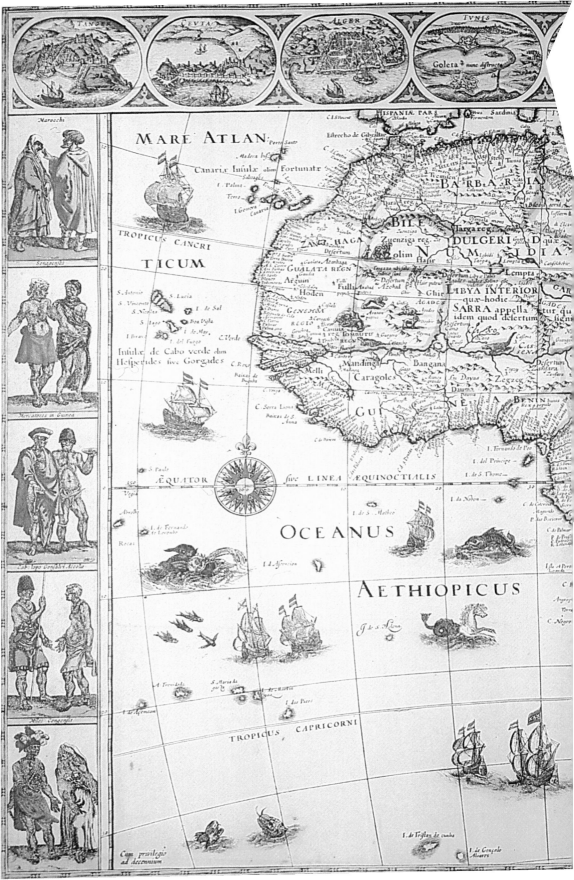

TANGER · **CEVTA** · **ALGER** · **TVNIS**

Goleta nunc destructa

Marocchi

Senegenfis

Mercatores in Guinea

Cap. lopo Gonfalvi Accola

Moles Congenfis

MARE ATLAN·

Porto Santo

Estrecho de Gibraltar

HISPANIÆ PARS

Madera Inf.

Canariæ Infulæ olim Fortunatæ

Salvages

I. Palma

Ferro

I. Gomara Canaria

TROPICUS CANCRI

TICUM

BARBARIA

BILE

DULGERI D

olim N U M I D I A

LIBYA INTERIOR
quæ hodie
SARRA appella
idem quod desertum

ZANHAGA

Defertum

GUALATA REGN

Azanhaga

Aæguan

Hoden

GENEHOA
REGIO

S. Antonio

S. Vincente

S. Nicolao

S. Iago

I. Brava

S. Lucia

I. de Sal

Boa Vifta

I. de May

I. del Fuego

C. Verde

Infulæ de Cabo verde olim
Hefperides five Gorgades

C. Roxo

Baixas de
Buduba

C. Verga

C. Serra Leona

Baixas de S.
Anna

C. de Bonas

Mandinga

Melli

Caragoles

GUI

BENIN

NEA

Bangana

Zegzeg

Dauma

I. Fernando de Poo

I. del Principe

I. de S. Thome

ÆQUATOR

S. Paulo

Vega

Abrolho

I. de Fernando
de Loronho

Rocas

five LINEA ÆQUINOCTIALIS

I. de Nobon

I. de S. Matheo

OCEANUS

I. d. Afcenfion

AETHIOPICUS

I. de S. Hæ Lena

TROPICUS CAPRICORNI

A. Trenidade

S. Maria de
que

A. de Martin

I. de Picos

I. de Agoman

I. de Trifian de cunha

I. de Gonçalo
Alvares